DIRT ROADS LEAVE RUTS IN YOUR SOUL

DIRT ROADS LEAVE RUTS IN YOUR SOUL

By

BILL LEE

ISBN: 1535025166
ISBN 13: 9781535025164

Dirt Roads Leave Ruts in Your Soul

For:

My Wife - Frances M. Lee
My Children – Ashley L. Hall, Abby L. Register, Anna M. Lee
My Grandchildren – Kayleigh, Kami, Kloe, Sam,
Marlaina, Tatum, Maddie and Landon (Willie Allen)
Siblings – Janis L. Johnson, Silas D. Lee

In Remembrance of:

Parents – James Quincy Lee and Gertrude M. Lee
Grandparents – Silas D. Lee and Mary Della Brock Lee
Extended Family – Uncle Homer Lee and Aunt Annie Rosa Lee
Many other family members, friends and community people from the
County Line Dirt Road and Bethel Primitive Baptist Church
Community

Special Thanks and Acknowledgements to:

Mr. Bobby Newsom for Cover Artwork
Ms. Dianne Smith for being a great English teacher a few years back and
Encouraging me to write the book
Gloria Pipkin for Assistance with Editing

TABLE OF CONTENTS

Chapter 1

DIRT ROADS LEAVE RUTS IN YOUR SOUL

If you have ever traveled down dirt roads on a regular basis, you know every trip leaves tracks in the dirt that are evidence of someone or something passing by. These tracks could be a foot print, bicycle track, or vehicle tire track. They could also be tracks from any number of wild animals such as squirrels, raccoons, opossums, deer, or snakes. I have even seen tracks left by an alligator making his way from one pond or creek to another in the dirt roads close to the old home place where I was raised. These tracks are very temporary in their existence and last only as long as the next traveler is passing by, the next vehicle leaving a new set of tracks, or the next rain to wash away any sign of something or someone having passed that way.

But if you have been a regular traveler on dirt roads, you also know there is another type of tracks in dirt roads that are long-lasting and often mark the way for those to follow. These are the areas of the roadway that are trampled down by repeated trips and often show the travelers the best path to take to avoid the many bumps that naturally occur on unpaved roads. As a dirt road is heavily traveled or maybe during times of heavy rain or storms, these long lasting tracks become more and more defined and sometimes even become the only possible path to take to reach one's desired destination. These well-defined paths are often referred to as ruts. And though these ruts can sometimes be muddy and rough, they are often deeper than the surrounding roadbed and may appear to be a less desirable trail to travel, they are in fact the best place to be when the roadway becomes treacherous.

Many times during my years of growing up with dirt roads with well-defined ruts leading to and from our home place, I was a witness to a traveler who had strayed from those ruts and bogged down or ended up in the ditch. As we were one of the families with tractors in our area, it was not uncommon for these stranded souls to come to our home seeking assistance in getting out of their predicament in order to continue on their travels. But if travelers follow the ruts, pay careful attention, and really understand that the ruts are the best path to take, then they are able to navigate the journey and reach their desired destination.

So it is with the ruts left in the dirt roads of my life by loved ones and family members who traveled before me. The ruts they traveled are deep and well defined. They clearly marked the best path to travel as I struck out on my own journey and have served me well over the years as I have moved on down the road. The ruts have helped guide me and show me which way to go. And, once in a while, just when I was about to go off into a ditch or get bogged down, I have been able to look for the ruts in the road, get back into them, and keep on going. And, when I have followed these ruts, they have always led me home.

When one considers the word *soul*, the idea or concept that often comes to mind is of the deepest part of one's being. The soul is the essence of the person, with core values, beliefs, and behaviors that define each of us. The ruts in my soul formed during the travels down those dirt roads of my past continue to guide me and provide a trail to follow. As the ruts in a dirt road are most of the time few in number but well defined, so too are those ruts in my soul that were well taught and demonstrated by those around me who had huge influences on my life as I grew up.

One of the ruts ingrained into me was that of a deeply held faith in God. This rut was demonstrated by deeds and actions of many of the adults around me. We were regular attendees and supporters of a little church of which my grandmother was a charter member. We prayed for one another, we said grace before our meals, and our family tried to live a life that would be pleasing to the Lord. But there was much more to this rut of faith developing besides outward, overt behaviors. For example, my dear Aunt Anne, who was our caretaker at home while my mother worked outside the home as a nurse, demonstrated inner peace and happiness better than any other person I have ever known. She trusted God to take care of her needs even though in human terms she had little reason to have this deeply held trust of faith. She was poor her whole life, never had many of the nicer things in life, and seldom if ever, had any luxury items in her home. Yet, she was always telling us children that God would provide a way. She taught us to just be happy in our station in life and told Bible stories about David, Samson, and Paul to teach us about faith and trust. My grandmother also had this same type of faith in God to provide for the needs of her family. My mother read the Bible often, was the one who made sure we went to church and even tried to make sure we paid attention while we were there. I must mention my older sister, Janis, who also was an influence on me as she was the first of us children to demonstrate a deeper understanding of faith when as a teenager, she made her own profession of belief in Jesus and joined the church. And, though my dad certainly was not the type of person to be at church every time the doors opened, he also made sure that we attended. He was a strong supporter of the ultimate message of faith: love one another, take care of your fellow man, and do good for others when you can.

Alongside of this rut in my soul comes another one that is closely related and well ingrained. This is the rut of family, honoring your parents and grandparents, providing for their needs, and supporting them in the good times and bad. This particular rut may be about as deep as any of these life markers. After all, I was raised on a farm that was homesteaded by my grandfather around 1912 and on which my family has resided continuously since then. My father and all of his siblings grew up on this farm. My Uncle Homer, who lived just up the dirt road from us, raised his family on this farm. My Aunt Ruby, another of the siblings, lived and raised her family just across another dirt road from this farm. My paternal grandparents, who were the homesteaders, lived less than 50 yards from the home I was raised in. We all lived close to each other, had very similar views of life, took care of one another, worked together in the gardens and fields and shared the produce with the extended family.

As my grandparents aged and moved toward the time in their lives of becoming more dependent on others, the family was always there to help meet their needs. Included in this was meeting their financial needs, providing for health care services, filling their freezer and pantry with food, transporting them to the places they needed to go such as the grocery store, the local farm supply store, or the doctor. There was, never to my knowledge, any type of indication that taking care of the needs of my grandparents was an issue. My parents and the other kin folks just did it. And, not only did they do it for this set of grandparents, but when my maternal grandmother and her husband reached the age of needing full time help, they moved into our home with us, and we just kept on giving and living.

My dad would often tell of the importance of protecting our family name and remind me that I was not just an individual but was a member of the Lee family. He expected us to conduct ourselves in a manner that would not bring embarrassment to the family. He also expected us to treat people--especially anyone that was our elder—with respect. Acknowledging your elders with a "yes sir" or "no sir," "yes ma'am" or "no ma'am" was not an option at our home. If you were overheard in an exchange with someone older than you and you failed to answer in a proper manner, Dad would be quick to say something like, "Boy, is your 'yes sir' broken?" The proper response was, "No, sir. Sorry, Mr. or Ms. Whoever."

The message of this rut was and is loud and clear. Take care of your family. Love them and attend to their needs as long as you are able to do so. And when you are not able to do so, then, to the best of your ability, provide whatever assistance you can to make sure they are taken care of in an appropriate and loving manner. Honor your parents and grandparents and respect your elders.

Work and earn your way in life was another of the ruts that was taught to me and my siblings. Goodness, how blessed I was to have had this rut plowed before me by my grandparents, parents, uncles, and aunts. My grandfather worked his whole life to earn a meager living, by today's standards, for his family. I remember him telling me he had worked many a day on the river pushing logs down to the mill for 50 cents a day. My grandmother picked vegetables, had chickens for eggs, and canned fruits and vegetables for sale to others. She would ride a wagon from her home to town in Bonifay (5 miles) and to Caryville (7 miles) to sell these goods to the little stores to be sold to others. To put it mildly, my grandparents worked.

Growing up on the farm, these people taught my father and his brothers and sisters to work. My mother, who was also raised on a small family farm, was taught by her dad and mom to work. My dad worked away from home as a sheet metal worker for much of his adult life and then worked in law enforcement for a number of years. He went to work each day and came home at the end of the day to his family, bringing whatever wages he earned each week home with him to provide for his family. My mother was a public health nurse for over 35 years. She did the same thing--went to work every day and whatever she earned, she brought home to help provide for her family. They worked.

When we were growing up, they taught us to work and provide for our family. My brother and I did farm chores like cutting wood, milking cows, or hoeing cotton and worked for other farmers in the area harvesting watermelons, peas, corn, cotton, hay, or whatever else might have been growing at the time. My sister helped with the inside chores of washing clothes, doing dishes, and cleaning the house. We were taught to work, and this rut has served all of us very well.

Though certainly not the last rut in my soul that I could discuss, one other that I feel is of importance was the rut of just treating people right. This was emphasized in many ways in our home. If people came to our home, they were treated with respect. If a meal was being served, everyone was invited to eat, no matter if they were expected for the meal or not. If there was not enough, more would be cooked. If someone had a need, my parents tried to help them if they could. If neighbors came looking for assistance with some type of farm chore or needed some type of metal work done, at which my dad was a highly skilled craftsman, he would just drop what he was doing and help. And I can't even begin to relate how many time my mother, a registered nurse, would be called late at night by some neighborhood family with a sick child or loved one seeking medical help, and Mother would get up and go check on the person with never any expectation of payment. Of course, I must say here that this same type of behavior was the norm for most of the folks who lived in our neck of the woods.

In considering the "ruts in my soul" as these described above, I suppose it would be a futile effort to list all of these ruts that are a part of my being. There would be too many and the length of the writing would be maybe a novel in length. Just suffice it to say that the ruts in the dirt road of my soul are an ever-present source of guidance as I travel down the road of life. These ruts always show me the best course to travel, especially in those stormy times we all encounter—and best of all, they always lead me home to the values and deeply held core beliefs in my soul.

I trust as I have lived my life and been blessed enough to have 3 wonderful children and 8 beautiful grandchildren (so far) that I have also been able to show them these same ruts to follow as they are on the dirt road of life.

As you read this and the other writings contained in this book, I hope you will be taken back home to the dirt roads of your own life. I hope some of these will cause you to reflect on your journey, to pause for a moment and recall some moment in time with loved ones and friends. I hope some of these will cause you to smile, chuckle, or even laugh out loud. Perhaps others will bring a tear to your eyes and will take you back to times that were challenging or trying. Or maybe the tears will be those of joy for some memory of loved ones, family, or friends during the great times of life.

One time when my daughter Anna was about 10 years old, I stepped into her bedroom and she was sitting in the middle of her bed, totally engrossed in a book she was reading. I stopped to chat with her about the book and she told me, "Dad, when I am reading this book, it is just like I am in the book with them."

With this thought in mind, when you are reading this book, I hope you will be there with me and will be able to just travel back to where the "Dirt Roads Have Left Ruts in Your Soul."

Chapter 2

THE BOY ON THE STEPS

The pictures included within this essay are of me as a young boy sitting on the back steps of the old family home where I lived for the first 5 plus years of my life. The home was constructed after my grandfather, Silas D. Lee and grandmother, Mary Della Brock Lee, homesteaded the land in about 1912. At the time the pictures were taken, 3 generations of the Lee family lived in the home including my grandparents, dad, mom, my sister Janis, my brother Silas and me.

In the first picture, I am eating some chocolate pudding or cake batter that either my mother, Aunt Anne, or Ma (grandmother) had given to me with not a care in the world except enjoying the delicious taste. That is but one hint of what life was like at the time this picture was taken for those living there at the time. The steps of the old house on which I am sitting while eating the chocolate pudding or cake batter served as the entrance way into the "shotgun" house with a great hall down the middle with rooms on each side. Looking closely at the top picture, one can see all the way through the house from back to front with screen doors on each end. The rooms were a kitchen and family room on one side of the hall and bedrooms on the other side. Each of these had fire places in them for heat during the winter and only windows and tall ceilings to al-low for air flow to help keep the house cool during the blistering heat of north Florida summers. The original house had no inside plumbing, i.e. bathroom, but one had been added to the house just a few years before the picture was taken.

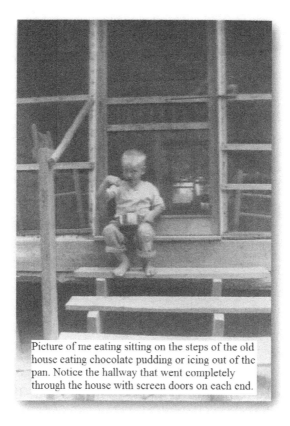

Picture of me eating sitting on the steps of the old house eating chocolate pudding or icing out of the pan. Notice the hallway that went completely through the house with screen doors on each end.

Prior to this addition of modern plumbing, the entire family made use of the "outhouse" for those necessary events of life, day or night, rain or shine, hot or cold. The old house gives another hint about the family that lived there. We were not the type of family or people who had a lot of the nicer things of life but we had the things we needed most. We had a long family history on the old home place which an-chored us to one another with a strong bond that had sustained us for many years and would continue to serve as an anchor for our family in the years ahead.

There is another hint in the picture that tells a lot about my family and me. If you notice, I appear to be very happy and would seem to feel very good about my place in life. Apparently, I have no concern about anything at all except to eat the chocolate pudding. It looks as if I am enjoying the beautiful day, barefooted as the day I was born, pants rolled up for a little cooling and not a worry in the world. I am absolutely secure in my surroundings. This feeling of security was evident on this day and was, in fact, the normal way of life for me in my family. I never had to worry about my dad, mom or extended family members who lived nearby to act in a manner that was irresponsible in any way as related to making sure that our needs, physical, emotional and spiritual, were met. It was a great place to be at the time of the pictures.

In the years ahead, these same qualities of life continued to be the norm for the Lee family out on Route 1, Bonifay, Florida. My grandpar-ents, mom and dad, and aunts and uncles with their families who lived close by all conducted their lives using a very common set of mores and standards in our little community. The people who lived with and around us were just good, hard-working, down-to-earth common folks who were conservative in their thoughts and actions, liberal in their willingness to help their neighbors, and strong in their faith in God. These people all lived by a creed of honesty, treating people "right", and love for their country. Most of the men in the neighborhood (and a few of the women including my mom) had been in the military during World War II and were proud to have served their country.

All of the children of these families were taught to work in various endeavors at their homes. Boys helped with the farming, tending of the animals and other outside chores, girls helped with the housework and inside chores and all of them helped with the processing of the food that was grown in the gardens at every home place.

Respect for grown folks was taught from an early age to all of us kids and disrespect to an elder person was quickly corrected if one of us had little enough sense to try such a foolish act. Yes sir, yes ma'am, no sir and no ma'am were not optional ways to respond to adults around our neck of the woods. Anything less than the above responses to a grown person were subject to be met with a swift reprimand to the offending party by any adult who was nearby whether they were our parents or not.

Saying grace before meals was the norm at every home especially at dinner (lunch) and supper (dinner). Sunday was a day of rest except for the rare times when some condition beyond the norm would necessitate some type of labor to be performed.

I feel I must also mention one other item from one of the pictures. In this picture, sitting just above me on the inside of the screen porch is my dad. This is a true representation of what he was to me for my entire life until he passed away. He was a constant in my life and was always watching over me and out for me and our entire family. He loved me and our family deeply though it was difficult for him to say this verbally. He was the rock of the Lee family and his influence was strong on all of us. He took the job of being the leader of our family seriously and tried his best to provide for us every day of his life. He was the source of many of my deepest held beliefs for how to be a man and a father. Many of the incidents in the following stories are about my dad, either directly or indirectly. Some of these are quite humorous, others are of a more serious nature and several will reveal aspects of his life that made a lasting impression on the young boy in the pictures that is still very much a part of who I am today.

Bill Lee at about 5 years of age on the steps of the old house with Dad (Quincy Lee) sitting in straight chair on the porch.

If somehow my mother had also shown up in the background of the pictures I would say that it would have been a perfect representation of all that I have been in my life. For I was truly blessed to have had great parents who loved me, watched out for me, wanted the best for me and tried in every way to ensure that I had every opportunity to be successful.

I have had many blessings in this life - a great wife, beautiful and talented children, wonderful grandchildren, good jobs, many friends, material blessings, and too many others to name. But, without a doubt, the one blessing that made all of the others possible was that I had a great daddy and momma that prepared me to travel down my own dirt roads.

Chapter 3

PA

I really believe if every child on earth had a "Pa" like I had when growing up, the world would be a much better place for all of humanity.

My Pa was my paternal grandfather. His name was Silas D. Lee and he was over 70 years old when I was born into the Lee family clan. I was the baby of the family and, even if I do say so myself, I was the apple of my Pa's eye. Don't get me wrong. This gentle, kind hearted man loved everyone in his family. He loved all of the grandchildren. But, he had a special place in his heart for the baby boy that was born late in his life.

My Pa was, as I said before, a kind and gentle man with a quick wit and smile for everyone. Though he passed away when I was only 13 years old, he taught me many things about life that still guide me today. My earliest memories of my Pa are of me sitting in his lap and him giving me what he called a "Joy Ride." For this, I would lie down in his lap, head toward his knees and feet at his stomach. He would bounce me up and down while giving me a gentle tickle on the ribs. He gave these joy rides to me until I had to let my legs hang down beside him, through the arms on his old rocker, and almost touching the floor. I only quit taking these joy rides because I outgrew his lap.

Pa spent quality time with me in my young childhood years, teaching me many things about life. He was the one that taught me how to shuck corn for the horse and mule that were on our farm. Feeding these was one of our jobs that we did together every day before I was old enough to start school. At feeding time, we would go out to the old crib where the corn that had been gathered was stored from year to year. I would crawl up in the crib, grab a feed bucket and fill it full of ears of corn.

We would take the time to shuck the husks off the ears of corn that we were going to feed to the horse and mule. Unknown to me at the time, the animals could have eaten the corn with the shucks on. But, Pa thought it was just the way that we needed to take care of these two animals that were housed in the horse stall, just a little way down the hill from the house. When finished shucking the corn, we would take it into the stall and divide it equally between Bob, the horse, and Daisy, the mule. While there, we would put fresh water in the trough. These feeding sessions were my first lessons in life on taking care of something (either animals or people) that could not take care of themselves.

My Pa also taught me to scull a boat. Now, for those who do not know what sculling a boat is all about, it is a way to use a boat paddle with one hand to propel a small fishing boat across a lake or up and down a stream. This is a very rare art in today's world as electric trolling motors have made this skill almost obsolete. But, when my Pa was teaching me, it was best way that a person could navigate a boat in a lake or stream with one hand and fish with a cane pole in the other hand.

Pa would take me down to our small farm pond and we would get in the boat. I would sit in the back seat and Pa would be in the second seat from the back. He would gently guide me in how to grip the paddle and place it in the sculling notch on the boat transom.

The motion needed to skull a boat is sort of like a horizontal figure 8, pushing and pulling the paddle from side to side while at the same time rolling the wrist to keep the proper angle on the paddle as it slices through the water. Using this technique, a person that knows how to skull a boat can cause a boat to move silently across a lake while hardly causing a ripple on the surface. It allows those skilled in this art to move into areas likely to have fish in them without causing any disturbance at all to the lake.

This lesson on sculling a boat was not one that was done in one or two days. Pa took me down to the pond many, many times before I was able to skull a boat with any degree of skill. Later, we would take some worms and poles with us and he would let me "run" the boat as we fished for the bream in the pond. These afternoons spent on the waters of our pond, fishing with my Pa, helped to develop my love of the outdoors that I still have to this day.

While growing up, Pa would tell me about the types of work that he had done as a younger man. He was a logger, working long, hard hours of manual labor to provide for his family. He even rode the logs down the river, as they did many years ago, to get them to the mills to be processed into lumber. He farmed and sold produce to area families to help provide for the financial needs of his wife and children. This ethic of working hard to provide for the needs of the family has been passed right on down to the generations that have followed.

One of the few vices that I remember that he had was that he smoked. Of course when he started smoking in the late 1800's, the dangers associated with it that are so well documented today were not known. As a matter of fact, many advertisements in magazines and newspapers of that time told of the health benefits of smoking. Hard to believe that smoking was once considered a healthy lifestyle choice.

Anyway, my Pa smoked Lucky Strike cigarettes. He preferred these over any other brand. If he could not get Lucky Strikes or if he ran out, he would smoke Chesterfield Kings. I remember him telling me that he started smoking at about the age of 14. As he was born in 1879, this was well before the beginning of the 20th century. He continued to smoke until shortly before his death at the age of 87.   Sadly, it was this lone vice that caused his death as he died from complications of emphysema in October of 1966.

I never remember seeing my Pa angry. From what my dad says though, he could get riled when the time called for it. I do recall a funny incident that happened when telephones were first coming into use in our area that did demonstrate that he could get a little steamed up when necessary. When my mom and dad got our first telephones out in the country, they had an extension run to my Pa and Ma's house, which was just about 100 feet from our house.

To fully understand this, I have to say that both of my grandparents were of the sure enough old school. They believed by word and action that the best way to live life was early to bed and early to rise. When dark came, no matter the time of the year, they were going to be in bed shortly thereafter. When the sun came up, it was time to get up and get busy. They did not believe in wasting daylight or using up too much of the dark.

On this particular night, our family was not at home. Don't remember if we had gone to visit friends or where we were, but we were not at home to answer the phone. My sister, who was a teenager at the time, had a number of her friends that also had telephones and one of them started calling our number, playing a trick on her or so they thought.   This was happening about 8:00 at night, a full couple of hours after my grandparents were in bed.

The friend would ring the number, my Pa would get up and get the telephone and nobody would say anything. He would hang it up and go back to bed. A few minutes later, the phone would ring again, he would get up to answer it, and no one would say anything. This happened about 4 or 5 times. Finally, my Pa had had enough.

The phone rang and Pa answered it one more time. Again, silence on the other end. This time though, instead of just hanging up, my Pa, in an agitated voice, said, "Well, why don't you just ring the son-of-a-b****? You can't talk no way!" That particular night, there were no more prank calls to the Lee household.   A couple of Janis' friends relayed this to her a few days later at school laughing their heads off at the shock they had received from Pa. In fact, there were no more prank calls to my sister again from this group of young folks.

My Pa, though not a person to get too excited very often, was a person of convictions. He believed what he believed and tried to live his life in a way to treat everyone right. But, if he ever had the occasion to believe that someone had wronged him or cheated him, then he marked that person off his list, so to speak. He would be kind to them, he would speak to them. But, he would not give them a second chance to do him or his family wrong.

I don't know if it is the genes that pass traits on from one generation to the next or if it is environment that does this or some combination of the two. But, I will say, this is one trait that my Pa had that was directly passed on to my dad, either by genes or by environment. I am afraid that I also have a pretty good dose of this in me, as do my sister and brother, also. Given this, I believe that I will just say it must be in the genes.

My Pa died when I was 13 years old. My parents sort of tricked me and asked me to watch a younger cousin outside of the church during the funeral service. I did not know why they did this at the time but I now know that they were afraid that I would be too upset during the funeral service of my Pa, a person that I loved dearly. They were probably right though I must admit that I have wished many times that I had gone into the church for the service.

As I have moved on through life, I have come to treasure the memories of my Pa more and more. I remember when I was a young adult and had grown to well over six feet tall and over 250 pounds that I wished my Pa could have been alive to see what a man I had become. I wish that he could have been there to see me marry and have children of my own. But, that is not the way of life.

However, whatever happens in this life, I will always know that my Pa loved me unconditionally and that I was special to him. He showed this love to me in many ways, mostly without having to say it verbally. I only wish that every child in the world could be so lucky to have a Pa like mine.

Life moves on. I now have my first grandchild. I hope that she knows how much I love her and treasure my time with her.

She calls me - Pa.

Note – Since writing this, we have added 5 more granddaughters and 2 grandsons to the Lee family. I love each and every one of them completely. They all call me Pa and it thrills my heart every time one of them says "Pa." to me or gives me a hug or spends time with me. I still hope that I am the Pa to them that my Pa was to me.

Paternal Grandparents
Silas D. Lee and Mary Della Brock Lee

Chapter 4

THE FIRST WORKAHOLIC I EVER KNEW!!

Without a doubt, the first honest to God, never to be questioned workaholic that I ever knew was Mary Della Brock Lee, better known to me as Ma, my paternal grandmother. She wholeheartedly believed that idle hands are the devil's workshop and she demonstrated this belief by word and deed everyday of her life or at least for the years that I knew her. Hearing my dad, my Uncle Homer and others in the family over the years discussing Ma and her ways, I am pretty sure that she was this way her whole life.

My Ma was a woman who always had something on her list of things to do that needed to be done by someone. She woke up every day, or so it seemed to me, with an endless list of chores that had to be done and done right quickly. Following is just a short list of some of the chores that she would have somebody doing if you were observed in her earshot with nothing to do.

In the spring or summer, she would put you to pulling pusley from the garden and taking it by the arm loads to the chicken yard to feed the laying hens and biddies (chicks). Pusley is a green plant that grows close to the ground in garden areas and is a nuisance weed. But to Ma, it was just another ready source of feed for her chickens, ready for the harvest.

All she needed to get it done was some idle hands and time. Children had plenty of both of these and she was always ready to supervise the work. It blame sure wasn't any fun to do this chore. The fact that it was work and not fun apparently just worried the heck out of Ma. Yeah, right!

Another chore that she would have you doing in a heartbeat was raking the yards. Not with a fancy, store bought yard rake either but rather a home-made goose berry yard broom. This crude instrument for cleaning yards was made by tying together a small bundle of goose berry limbs with the leaf ends on the bottom and the stems at the top. When tied together tightly, the rake would be about 3 or 4 inches in diameter at the top end and about 10 or 12 inches down close to the ground. It was a crude rake, at least by today's standards but it would clean a yard of any and all leaves and debris.

Ma didn't want any leaves in the yard gathering up and blowing around. As our old home place was right in the middle of 4 huge clusters of oak trees, this was a problem year around. But it was especially a problem in the fall of the year when leaves were shedding and in the spring when the trees were blooming. I can still hear her calling the names of my brother, my cousin and me to start raking them dang leaves when we were not quite quick enough to be out of her eyesight before she caught us. I still do not like raking leaves!

If these chores were completed or didn't need to be done, she would send you to start chopping fire wood for her wood stove. She cooked on a wood stove until shortly before her death even though my parents had bought her an electric stove several years earlier. The old wood stove required small pieces of wood to burn in the stove and these had to be chopped on a regular basis. This was one of those chores that you never got caught up on. Today there was firewood but tomorrow more will be needed. I dang sure don't like to chop wood today, either.

I could go on and on listing the chores that my Ma would have you doing. Gardening, grinding chops for the biddies, feeding and watering the laying hens, washing vegetables from the garden, shelling peas or but-terbeans, hoeing the garden, …..the list is non-exhaustive.

The best defense for this workaholic lady was to stay out of her eye-sight and out of earshot.   If she saw you and you weren't busy, it was too late. She could and would *find* you something to do if you looked the least bit like you were available.

Now reading this, you might think that this lady was tough on those around her.   But, as Paul Harvey says, you need to know the rest of the story.

My Ma was a workaholic, no doubt. But, it was because she loved her family. In her younger years, she would leave home shortly after dawn, ride a mule and wagon over to Caryville to peddle garden vegetables to the people working in the saw mills to make money to feed and clothe her children. She would return home late in the day and go to the garden to gather another round of vegetables for the trip the next day. She would then go in and cook supper for her five children and husband and get them ready for bed.

On the days that she didn't go to peddle her goods, she would be at home, washing clothes in an old wash pot using homemade lye soap and water heated with wood chopped by her or her sons. If it wasn't wash day, she would be canning food, making quilts, sewing clothes out of feed sacks or some other task to keep her family fed and clothed. In the early days of her life, when her own children were small, it was the only way she was able to survive.

Did this way of life frame her whole lifetime of work? It did, without a doubt. Am I really, deep down thankful for this? Without a doubt, I am. For you see, this work ethic was passed on to at least three generations that have followed her example. The example set by her (and my Pa, her husband) of working to earn an honest living has been the foundation of our entire family. All of her children were successful adults. Her grand-children, or at least the huge majority of them, have always worked hard to earn an honest living. The great grandchildren, at least the ones that I know about, are all now hardworking adults who continue to live out this legacy of an honest day's work for an honest day's pay. I believe that this legacy goes back to my Ma.

Thank God for her and for her workaholic ways.

Chapter 5

A FEW THINGS ABOUT DAD AND MOM

Mom and Dad on their 50th wedding anniversary.
One of the rare pictures of my dad in a suit.

He was a man who made many deals with a shake of the hand or on his and another person's word. He would write you off if you did not hold up your end of the bargain. Lived by the code of once burned was enough.

She was more of the live and let live personality and would give most folks more than one chance to mess up though she could also get a little testy with folks who did not hold up their end of the bargain.

He would give the shirt off his back to help someone in need and would not give the time of day to a person who was a user or someone who leeched off others. She was also a giver by nature and made this part of her personality a large part of her life's work as a public health nurse trying to meet the health needs of the rural people in Holmes County for over 35 years.

He loved to pull a good practical joke on others and would be the first to laugh and enjoy it when someone else pulled a good one on him. But he would always respond with, "You know that is going to cost you!" while he was laughing. He *would* pay you back when the opportunity presented itself.

She would just holler when dad pulled a joke on her. Would act like she was mad but before long, she would be laughing. She rarely got the best of dad in these exchanges but, when she did, she really enjoyed it.

He was totally politically incorrect his whole life or at least the portion of his life that I knew him. He did not waiver on his convictions, would not change just to please, and would speak his mind. She was much more inclined to temper her comments in sensitive situations though I do not recall that she ever compromised her beliefs. She probably used this ability to her advantage over the many years in public service work.

He knew how to use the fewest words possible to express his thoughts on a particular subject. In other words, people did not have to spend a whole lot of time trying to interpret what he meant or what he was trying to say in most situations. She would use more descriptive language in expressing herself when talking with others. She also said a few things that were always funny to me. As an example, she could never say the word "weird." No matter how hard she tried, she would pronounce this word phonetically as "wer–rid."

He was a life-long, yellow dog Democrat. As in he would vote for a yellow dog before he would vote for a Republican. He told me he had never voted for a Republican in his life. I have no reason to doubt this as we had many discussions over the years about political matters, world events, local elections and such. He never wavered in his opinion that Democrats were for the little man and Republicans were for the rich folks. She voted her convictions for the person seeking office though she also leaned towards being more Democrat than Republican. But, she would not talk politics much with those people outside a very closely held circle of family or friends. I guess she just thought that was one of those things in life that was a personal matter not for public discussion.

They both were hard core patriots who loved their country each having served in the military during World War II. He was in the Navy and she was in the Army. He was in the south Pacific on the island of Tinian when the bombers carrying the atomic bombs flew to Japan from the island of Saipan, which was only a few miles from Tinian and visible across the ocean. He was training up on the side of a mountain to be a part of the invasion force when word came that Japan had surrendered. She never went overseas but instead tended to the wounded soldiers returning home in an army hospital in Atlanta, Georgia.

He was not particularly religious on the outside but lived by the teachings of the Bible daily in his life – do good for your fellow man, help others in needs, take care of the needy, be honest in your dealings with others, treat others as you would have them you, honor your father and mother. She was much more outward in her religious beliefs, reading the Bible often that sat on the table by her easy chair and attending church often at her own church and with others. The last words that I remember her saying as she slipped into a coma preceding her passing away was quoting the 23rd Psalm.

He did not have much patience for people who made a point of acting like or telling people they were church-going folks but who were less than what they professed to be in their personal actions. She was more forgiving of human frailties and often said, "There but for the grace of God go I."

He did not like to go to church but loved to listen to gospel music, would travel to various places to hear gospel music and would tear up and cry as he listened to the songs about Jesus, the Lord, and God. She also loved gospel music and would accompany him on the trips.

He loved his family and was the stalwart for his family and the extended family from the time he returned from the Navy after World War II until he died. Though he was the acknowledged "captain of the ship", she was the glue that held it all together. And believe me, sometimes when necessary, she would put a course correction on the captain which would tighten the sails up for a while.

He was both hard-headed (wow, was he hard-headed) and tender hearted which is sort of an odd combination of personality traits. Once he locked down about an issue, there was no changing his mind unless he was absolutely convinced without doubt that there was some compelling reason to do so. She was also tender hearted but not sweet, which is also sort of an odd combination of personality traits. She had a real heart to help those in need but was more about meeting the need at hand than making sure she was being sweet to those around her. I would say she was a kind person who was aware of the feelings of others but she was not just naturally sweet.

He would cry at the drop of a hat over something bad happening to a loved one or close friend and could not attend a family gathering without his eyes filling with tears as he would try to talk about how much his family meant to him, especially as he and his brothers and sisters became older. She also really loved her family, being one of 11 children. She really enjoyed visiting with her brothers and sisters and their families in Panama City, Pensacola, Port St. Joe and with those who lived closer to our family home. Our annual family reunions also meant a lot to both of them.

We did not miss these while growing up and even after us children were grown, we were, how should I say this, expected to be in attendance.

He really enjoyed planting a garden, not so much gathering that which he had planted. But he would do it as needed. He was also good at processing the food grown in the gardens and could can, freeze, or preserve any of it for later use. He was really good at preparing fruits, jellies, jams, and was a master maker of home-made sugar cane syrup. He was also known to make some of the best peach brandy and grape wine in our area, for personal consumption only, of course.

She helped with the gardening a little bit and helped a lot with the canning, freezing and preserving. But, she was the best in the world at cooking the foods grown in the garden. A country meal of peas, corn, fried okra, sliced tomatoes, a few cucumbers, fried pork chops or country fried steak with a homemade pie for desert prepared by my mom was as good as it could get for food. Wish I could have one more of her home cooked meals.

He drove Chevrolet trucks. Not Fords, not Dodges, not GMCs. Chevrolets only. She drove Mercury cars. She did buy a Chevrolet Impala one time when she traded cars. Within just a few weeks of buying this car, she started expressing regret. Just as soon as if was feasible for her to do so, she traded the Chevrolet in and bought a Mercury. She owned a white, Mercury Marquis when she passed away. Hope they have some Mercury cars in heaven if they drive cars up there.

He was an expert quail hunter and bird dog trainer and loved to shoot dove. She was an expert seamstress and loved to be at her sewing machine. She made many of our clothes when we were young children and continued to make clothes for Janis into her teenage years.

He could make just about anything out of metal having been trained in metal works in the Navy. He was an expert welder and could not only weld plain old steel but also stainless steel and aluminum, which is very hard to do. I wish I had learned more about this from him.

My dad loved my mom and our family. It was hard for him to say this. I don't know why. He expressed many times that he was proud of our family and would tell us to make sure we protected our family name when we would be out and away from home. It was a good life lesson. He really missed my mom after she passed away and was lonely in the home they had shared for over 50 years. He was a great dad who also made sure that all of our needs and a whole lot of our wants were provided.

Mom really loved my dad and our family. Once in a while, she would sneak up on him and plant a big ol' kiss on his cheek or forehead while he would be sitting at the kitchen table or in his recliner. He would make some funny face or sound, acting like he did not want her to do that. But, you could tell that he really did like for her to show a little love to her man. She was a great mother who always wanted the best for her children and sacrificed many times and in many ways to provide for our needs and our wants.

He knew a lot of people and was friends to many. But, he had a life-long friend by the name of James Boswell who was special in many ways. They hunted together. They fished together. They laughed when they got together. They would help one another in times of need. They probably shared life's troubles with one another. They raised families at the same time and our entire families were friends. We camped out together. The families visited each other often when people still did that sort of thing. Mr. Boswell got sick and was nearing the time when he would pass away. My dad asked me to take him to visit Jim, as dad called him. They talked, they shared fond memories of times past, they laughed and they just enjoyed the time together. When we left, my dad was very quiet as we drove away. I saw the tears in his eyes and rolling down his face. I felt the tears run down my face also. My dad loved Jim Boswell. He did not have to say so.

As I have matured and been able to reflect on the times of my life, I have come to appreciate my parents and the lives they lived while on this earth more each day. They were good people. They loved their family. They were good neighbors. They helped people in need. They were people of principle and their word could be trusted. They taught their children to live by these same principles. I thank God every day for having had them as my mom and dad.

Chapter 6

FIRST SUNDAY – TIME FOR CHURCH

At Bethel Primitive Baptist Church, where my family attended church when I was a child, we had church only on the first Sunday of each month. This worship schedule was mainly because the pastor of our church was also the pastor for three other small churches in northwest Florida, southeast Alabama, and southwest Georgia. And since my grandmother was a charter member of Bethel, this was where we were going to go to church.

For the truly committed who attended Bethel; there was also a service on the Saturday night before first Sunday and sometimes on third Saturday night. This Saturday night meeting was often the time that the business of the church was conducted in a meeting called "conference." I must confess, I don't remember that, as a child, I attended many of these extra opportunities for worship.

Church meetings only once a month seemed like a pretty good deal at the time, particularly to a young boy raised in the country who was a lot more interested in free time to play than sitting in church. After all, there were many activities in which a young boy could become involved other than going to church. There were dams to be built across small streams, ball games to be played, calves to be ridden, fish to be caught, and swimming holes waiting.

Having only one Sunday per month occupied by church to interfere with such activities sure seemed like the best deal around at the time. After all, some of my uptown friends had to go to church every single Sunday. And, on top of that, they also had "Sunday School." Wasn't school bad enough during the week? Why in the world would anyone want to mess up Sunday by having to go to school again? I was glad to be going to Bethel.

On church Sunday at Bethel, we had three main activities. First we had singing, then we had preaching, then we had eating. On the first Sunday of every month, mom would get up, start stirring around, and begin getting us ready for church. We would wake up, have a good breakfast and dress in our Sunday clothes, and get ready to go. While we were doing all of this, my mom would also be cooking the food that we were going to take with us for the lunch meal after church.

Every family that attended church at Bethel would bring dinner with them to the church, packed away in containers of many kinds. Some would bring cardboard boxes that contained the food. Some would have fancy store- bought picnic baskets complete with matching plates and tea glasses. Some might have their food packed in Tupperware containers; others might have their food still in the boilers and pots that it had been cooked in. However, there was one thing in common among all the food that was brought and shared among those in attendance—it was delicious.

Before I get ahead of myself, let me describe how a day at church would usually go. Families would begin arriving at the church at about 9:30. Singing began at 10:00 or thereabouts. In the primitive Baptist faith, there is no instrumental music. So, all of the songs sung by the congregation are *a cappella*. Songs would begin with the leader, usually a man, humming to get the people on key. Then, he would begin the song and the rest of the congregation would join in. Most of the time most of the people would be mostly on key.

Some of the old familiar hymns, such as "Amazing Grace," "The Old Rugged Cross," and "Leaning on the Everlasting Arms," were sung beautifully in four-part harmony with few missed notes. However, there were times that it sounded as though everyone was doing their own thing, musically speaking, especially on the less familiar hymns. These were often an exercise in searching for the right notes by everyone in attendance, or so it seemed. When the sopranos would be right on key, the altos would be flat. Or maybe the bass singers would be right on target and the tenors would be just a tad sharp. In spite of these occasional musical challenges, I remember that the singing of these hymns was from the heart, to the glory of God, regardless of the less than perfect harmony.

The singing portion of the day usually ended at about 11:00. It was time for the preaching to begin. Most Sundays, there would be at least two preachers for the morning service. Sometimes, there would be three, but rarely do I remember it being just one. Maybe the thought was, if we just get one shot at these folks one time a month, we better at least double up or triple up on the preaching of the Word. Now the order for preachers was this; the visiting preacher (or preachers) went first, the pastor went last. And at Bethel Primitive Baptist Church, for a period of over 60 years, the pastor who got the last word was Elder C. W. (Carlton) Todd.

Most of the time, these sermons were of the real fire and brimstone variety. They were from the hearts of the preachers and were usually full of emotion. I can vividly remember many times as a boy wondering "Why do them preachers have to be so dad gum loud?" This was without the benefit of any PA system, too! Preacher Todd would follow the lead sermon, and his messages would often be of the more pastoral type, meant to help lead the flock to better lives by being more obedient to the Word.

As a side note, he was a great pastor for our little church. He loved the people of our community deeply and was a person who really showed his love for God by the way he lived his life. He baptized many in our community, including me at the age of 14, in the cold waters of Holmes Creek at the Vernon Park.

After the preaching was done, it was time for the eating. For some of us, this was about the best time of the day—we were going to get to eat some of the best food in the world, bar none! First Sunday, Dinner-on-the-Ground, After Church eating time was a feast fit for kings. And, as this was taking place at a church in the Deep South, it was more than fit for a whole passel of pure country rednecks.

The food that was prepared by these great Southern cooks and brought to church for everyone to enjoy defies adequate description. There was always plenty of fried chicken, pots of chicken and dumplings, hams, pot roast, and many other kinds of meats. There were vegetables of all kinds, fresh from the local gardens of church members. In the spring, new potatoes, English peas, and string beans were on the menu. A little later in the spring and summer, sweet corn, both on the cob and creamed, peas, okra, and home-grown tomatoes would be included in many baskets. In the fall and winter, turnip greens, cabbage, mustard greens, and collards would show up. And all throughout the year, home-made cornbread, biscuits, and hoecakes added enjoyment to the meals.

In addition to the seasonal foods that were prepared, almost every family had one or two cooks who prepared their special dishes for every first Sunday dinner. My mom prepared the best creamed corn in the world. When she fixed this, it was always one of the first bowls to be emptied. Though creamed corn is a pretty simple item to cook and it may seem that most of it would taste the same, this is not the case. My mom's was the best. Maybe it was just that extra little bit of love that she added was what made it so good.

My great aunt, Odee Harrell, always made egg custard pies that would just melt in your mouth. My Aunt Anne Lee would cook the best chicken and dumplings on earth. Some of the ladies would cook turnips complete with the roots added and pot liquor that would require at least two and sometimes three helpings. Others would cook field peas, rutabagas, and fresh squash, both stewed and fried.

And, if you had any room left after the main meal was finished, there were desserts galore. Pies of every kind, including pecan, pumpkin, potato, and blueberry, would be on the table. Coconut, pound, chocolate, lemon-cheese, and peanut butter cakes, among many other kinds, would be there for the taking and enjoying. If you didn't want any pie or cake, then you could choose from many other kinds of sweets such as banana pudding, vanilla pudding, or blueberry delight. One of the great things about this for me and the other boys and girls in attendance was that we could eat all we wanted of any of the foods available, including desserts.

At the completion of the meal, the adults would gather up the leftovers, pack the baskets, sit around and visit a little, and get ready for the trip home. The youngsters would go walking around the church grounds, maybe go out into the cemetery where loved ones were buried, being careful not to step on or over a grave, or walk down into the pasture until it was time to go home. Shortly parents would begin to call up their children, the leftovers would be loaded, and one by one, the folks would head home. On the drive home, conversations would turn to how the day had been, someone would comment on how good some particular food item had been, and one of the adults might comment on the sermon.

First Sunday Church was over. Four more weeks before we would do it again. Four more weeks before I had to sit through the church service. Four more weeks until I would get to eat some more of that great food.

Most of the older generation of people who attended church at Bethel have gone the way that all must go. They are now, we pray, having church every day. What a change for them in their church schedule! My mom, who passed away in December 2000, is one of these folks.

As I look back, Bethel was the place where I began my own faith journey. It was the place where I first felt the spirit of God speak to me. It was a place where friends, families, and loved ones gathered for fellowship and worship. It was also a place that had great food each and every first Sunday for all of my growing up years.

I wish I could have some more of my mom's creamed corn on first Sunday at Bethel Church one more time.

Chapter 7

PLANTING POTATOES

It is almost February 14. This date is universally recognized as Valentine's Day, the day of love, of candy and flowers, of romance and love. This day is viewed by many as the most "romantic" day of the year.

But, out in the country in the Deep South, this day is known for something as important as all of those things. For this date, February 14, is the traditional day for planting Irish potatoes in the South. There is really nothing romantic about this day because it is usually a day of work. It was on this day that the freshly plowed dirt in the garden was tilled and ready for planting. It was on this day that a season of renewal began. It was on this day that the sowing, tending, and reaping of the treasures of the earth began again.

At the Lee farm, on February 14 of any year, potatoes were going to be planted. The only two things that would interfere with this were if it was pouring rain or the 14th fell on a Sunday. Other than those two events, my grandmother, Della Brock Lee, was going to see potatoes going into the ground. As this day approaches, my memories take me back to our family farm in the panhandle of Florida. The dirt has been prepared by my dad or my uncle and the ground plowed in preparation for the "laying off of the rows," which was the only type of tilling of the soil required on planting day.

This was done in one of two ways: either they used the Farmall Cub, a very small tractor suitable only for garden work, or our old mule, Daisy. The use of the tractor was more common the older that Daisy (and my dad and my uncle) became. However, all of the boys in the family were taught to plow with the mule, just in case there was ever a time that a tractor wasn't available and we needed to plant a garden the old-fashioned way. After all, my parents were raised during the Great Depression, and they were convinced that days like the Depression might come again and there would be no gas to run a tractor. So, in the event that the "Hoover Days" came again, we learned to plow with the mule.

We had to know how to put the mule collar on ol' Daisy, connect the plow lines, attach the stock to the mule, change the type of plow blade to be used, and plow a reasonably straight row before we were declared graduates of "Mule Plowing 101." Unless you have ever tried to plow a mule, complete with all voice commands like *gee* (go right), *haw* (go left), *geddup* (get up or go), and *whoa* (stop) while walking quickly behind a mule over rough ground, keeping a plow running straight all the time, I am not sure that I can adequately explain how difficult this may be.

For those that have ever tried to operate a floor waxing machine, it is somewhat like that. You can't muscle a mule-drawn plow around too much. It requires an understanding of how it is done and a firm but gentle hand on the plow. Lean the plow stocks a little bit one way or the other, and the plow would take off in the opposite direction. And believe me, it could get away from you in a hurry. Let's just say that learning to plow with a mule was not one of those activities that you mastered the first few times you tried it.

After the ground was prepared, next came the dropping of the potatoes. This is the process where the potato buds are placed in the rows. As long as my grandmother (Ma) was alive, there was only one way that this could be done correctly. The potato buds had to be placed in the rows "eyes up." If Ma found potatoes that had been dropped "eyes down" in a row, somebody was going to be in trouble.

The eye of the potato is the part from which new plants emerge. Scientifically speaking, it does not make one bit of difference if the buds are placed "eyes up," "eyes down," or "eyes sideways." The new plants are going to grow toward the warmth of the surface and toward the sun. But to Ma, there was only one way to do it—"eyes up."

What is really funny about this though is how my father supported Ma in this "eyes up" planting philosophy. He knew that the way the potatoes were placed in the rows did not make any difference in what kind of potato crop would be produced. Yet, when Ma was in charge of the garden planting, as she was until her death, he went along with her on making sure that the potatoes were planted "eyes up."

Oh, occasionally, when she walked out of earshot, he might grumble a little and say, "It don't make a damn which way them potatoes are dropped as long as they are covered right." But, if she was close by and supervising, which was often, he made sure to support her in her demand that they be planted "eyes up."

I did not really understand then why he did this knowing that it did not make any difference. Maybe he just didn't want to hear the griping. Maybe it was just easier to go along than to argue with Ma, who was, to say the least, a little headstrong. But in thinking about this over the last few years, I believe he did this because of his deep love and respect for his mom.

He did it because of his deeply held conviction that parents deserved the respect of their children, no matter their age. He did it because he had come to understand that his mom, in spite of her stubbornness, was convinced that she was right and was deserving of support. He did it to help teach us children that respect for parents has no age limit. These were all lessons well taught and well learned.

As an adult now, I am so thankful that I lived on a farm and learned about planting potatoes. I am glad that my grandparents and parents allowed me to experience things in life like planting gardens, smelling the freshly tilled earth, working with my hands, and even plowing a mule, which I have (thankfully) not had to do in the last 30 or so years.

But most of all, I am thankful for being taught that respect for parents, grandparents, other adults and children, has no age limit. I am thankful that my dad taught by example to "honor thy father and thy mother." I am glad that one of the values that I hold deeply as one of the foundations of my life is that respect for parents is just the right thing to do. Obviously, I did not know this was being taught at the time that it was happening.

I just thought we were planting potatoes.

Chapter 8

CADILLAC MOTEL

N ot just any old motel but the **CADILLAC MOTEL**! That was the name of the very first motel I ever stayed in. It was located in Fanning Springs, Florida, right beside the Suwannee River and the trip that allowed this overnight stay was special.

One of the facts of life growing up in my family was that we did not take traditional family vacations where we would go on a road trip for several days to some great and fabulous place. There were probably many reasons for this, not the least of which was that we were not a family of great financial means. We lived on a small farm that my grandfather had homesteaded many years before, and it required a lot of time on the part of my parents to keep it going. Also, because traditional family vacation time comes during the very heart of farming season, it made vacations pretty low in the order of importance.

Most of our "vacations" consisted of short trips to visit some of our many relatives that lived in other area towns. And, since my mom had 10 brothers and sisters that lived in places like Panama City, Pensacola, and Port St. Joe, there were always some of them that had not been visited in a while. Most of these short trips visiting aunts, uncles, and cousins would last a couple of days, maybe three, and then we would head back home to the farm.

But, on this one special occasion, my mother decided to take a trip to visit some relatives that lived all the way down in the Tampa area, which was a long way from our Bonifay, Florida, home in the early 1960's. Going on this trip was my mother, my sister Janis, my brother Silas, my Aunt Dola, and me. We headed out, with the plans to see some of the tourist sites along the way between Bonifay and Tampa as well as visit kinfolk upon arrival.

One of these stops became a memory of laughter and good times to all of us on this trip. As we were headed south on U.S. 98, we went through a small community named Salem. Just before we passed through Salem, we saw a very small roadside zoo that my siblings and I wanted to visit, but, my mom didn't want to stop. As children are prone to do, we kept on begging and finally she relented, turned around, and headed back to the zoo. We had to pass through Salem again to get back to the zoo. This made two trips through Salem.

After the zoo visit, we headed south, going through Salem for the third time that day. Just a few miles down the road, my sister realized that she had left her small camera on the counter in the zoo where she had pur- chased some film. One more time, we turned around and headed north, passing through Salem for the fourth time. We retrieved the camera from the zoo shop and headed south again, going through Salem for the fifth time in one day. We all began to laugh about whether or not we would ever be able to leave Salem and proceed on our trip. For years afterward, anytime some of us would be involved in something that amounted to going around in circles, invariably someone would ask, "Are you going through Salem?" and we would immediately know what they were talk- ing about.

Anyway, as we went along on our trip, the time approached when we needed to find a place to spend the night. As we came into the very small town of Fanning Springs, hard by the Suwannee River, my mom saw the Cadillac Motel and decided that it looked like a good place to stay. It was a neat little roadside inn that appeared to be clean and affordable. For my brother, sister, and me, it also had one other great feature—a real, honest-to-goodness cement swimming pool complete with diving board.

By today's standards, the Cadillac Motel was a basic one-star motel. Heck, even by standards in the 1960's, it was probably a basic one-star motel, if there was such a thing back then. But, in the eyes of a 7 or 8 year old boy from the farm, spending his first night in a motel with a pool, it was a fabulous resort.

We checked in and within two minutes, all of us children were in the pool. After all, except for the very rare times that we had gone to Chuck and Eddie's, a local bar with a pool that allowed the school to use it for summer recreation programs, our swimming experiences had been limited to the local creeks and lakes close to our home. We stayed in the pool until the manager made us get out at about 10:30 or 11:00. We all looked like some over ripe prunes, with enough wrinkles that left us looking as if we needed ironing. We all slept really well in the Cadillac Motel that night.

The next morning, we got up and proceeded on our trip. To be honest with you, I do not remember many of the other things about this trip other than some of the places we visited such as Silver Springs and Six Gun Territory near Ocala and the Singing Tower at Bok Tower Gardens in Lake Wales. We also went to a place known as Spook Hill, which is a hill that has an optical illusion to it that allows a car that is parked at what appears to be the bottom of a hill to roll up the hill when left in neutral.

Since then, as an adult, I have had the occasion to spend many nights in motels. These motel visits have been on business trips and vacations with my family. There have been one-night stays and week-long vacations. They have been at the beach, in the mountains, in New York City and at luxurious golf resorts. But, I really do not remember any of these like I remember the Cadillac Motel.

It must be in the name. After all, how can you beat a Cadillac? Either that or maybe it was just one of those memories about a time in life of simple joys and new adventures surrounded by loved ones that make life worth living and remembering.

Chapter 9

PICKIN' COTTON

Pickin' cotton, the old fashioned way, by hand, is one of those jobs on a farm that is just plain work. Nothing fancy needed to describe the process except to say that it is just hot, back-breaking, hard work.

Growing up on the Lee family farm in Holmes County, Florida, hard beside the county line dirt road that ran the border between Holmes and Washington counties, had many advantages. We were loved by a large, extended family that included parents, grandparents, aunts and uncles and cousins by the dozen. We enjoyed the fun times of farm life greatly, such as swimming in Holmes Creek during the summer, fishing in the creek, Choctawhatchee River or area lakes, and eating those wonderful country meals of fresh vegetables such as peas, cream corn, okra, and home-grown tomatoes.

But, there were also some times on the farm that served to remind one of what farm life was really about in the Deep South for many years. These days and times helped you to really appreciate the good times even more because you remembered that you could be doing something else. And, this something else didn't necessarily have to be fun. One such activity was picking cotton.

Planting cotton was one of those endeavors that my dad and Uncle Homer undertook to try and scratch a little bit of money out of the farmland. It was not unlike other similar activities that small family farmers of our area did to try and make ends meet. It began in the spring with the planting, progressed through the summer with the cultivation process, and ended in later summer with the harvest.

When the cotton was being planted on our farm, there was still a cotton allotment in place. An allotment is when the federal government sets a limit on how much of a certain crop a farmer is allowed to grow. This allotment is determined by a formula based on several factors, such as the total acreage of a farm and the size of the allotment in previous years. These allotments were designed with the intent of helping to hold prices steady by limiting the production of any particular product and not allowing a glut or overproduction to happen and prices to fall. Peanuts were another crop that was subject to these allotments.

The cotton allotment on our family farm was not very large, maybe about 10 acres or so. When the county agent would come by and check the acreage for compliance with the allotment, he would sometimes find out that my dad and uncle had planted a little too much. When this was the case, they had to plow up the amount over the allotment. In essence, the seed and fertilizer used in the planting of the amount over the allotment was wasted. By the way, I sure am glad that our allotment was this small because this was plenty big enough for me.

The planting was about like all other crops. The ground was prepared by disking and breaking up the land. The fertilizer was added to the soil and the seeds were planted. Along with this went some praying for the right kind of weather, especially for the first few weeks, so that the seed would properly germinate and a good stand of cotton would be obtained. After the seeds were in the ground, it was just wait and see if the cotton would come up.

A few weeks into the growing of the cotton came the first really bad job associated with the production of the cotton crop—hoeing the cotton. This job was done with my Uncle Homer serving as the foreman of the crew and my brother Silas, my cousin Sammy, and me doing the hoeing. This job usually lasted several days and had to be done at least of couple of times during the growing season. Once the last hoeing was completed, the cotton was left to grow to maturity.

In thinking back on this process of hoeing the cotton, it occurred to me that my dad must not have heard of using herbicides for the control of weeds. Maybe it was because he had some home grown herbicides at his farm. These herbicides had names like Silas, Sammy, and Bill. Perhaps the reason that he did not use store-bought herbicides was that they would cost money he didn't want to spend. Beside, in his mind, he was already footing the bill for the home-grown herbicides he was using.

As the cotton moved toward maturity, the bolls would begin to open, displaying one of the more beautiful sights in the farm industry. When I think of images of farms in America, in my mind I either see a golden wheat crop flowing in the wind of a Midwest field or I see a white cotton field in the Deep South. Both of these images remind us that all of America owes a great debt to those in our great country who have been involved in agriculture over the years. It is a part of my heritage of which I am very proud.

It is now late summer and the cotton crop has matured. The bowls of cotton are open on all the stalks. The cotton gleams pure white in the late summer sun. Let the fun begin.

When my family was growing cotton, we did not use any mechanical harvesters or cotton pickers. These machines were available, but we did not have access to one. Besides that, my dad had seen where these machines were used and he thought they wasted a lot of cotton by leaving it in the field. He was convinced that the best way to harvest the crop was the old fashioned way—by hand picking it.

When the harvest began, my dad would go to town and round up whoever was willing to work in the field to pick the cotton. He would use the old farm truck with a set of high bodies in the back to bring the workers back. In the late 1950's to early 1960's, most of these who worked to pick the cotton on our farm were black men and women and their children, along with those in our immediate families who lived on the farm.

The cotton harvest would begin late in the month of August before the new school year began. The work day would begin early and last until almost sundown. The going rate for this backbreaking labor of picking the cotton was 3 cents a pound. That's right! Three cents a pound!! This meant that if you were able to pick 100 pounds of cotton in a day, which was very difficult to do, you would earn the large amount of $3.00.

The pickers always wanted to start just as early as they could in the morning. This was because the dew was still on the cotton, and the cotton would weigh out heavier while this moisture was on it. After the sun came up and dried the dew, the cotton would be fluffy and light and it would not weigh as much. Pickers were always trying their best to pick as many pounds as they could each day. As they would fill up a bag, they would take it to the barn to be weighed on the cotton scales. After my mom or dad recorded the weight, the picker would grab a new bag and head back to the field.

Once in a while, a picker who was trying to pull a fast one would throw a citron (immature or mutated watermelon) in the bottom of the picking bag and then fill it the rest of the way with cotton. A cittern grows wild in fields and is not any good to eat, though cows and hogs will eat them. Adding this weight to a cotton bag would add 8 to 10 pounds to the amount that would be credited to a picker. If my dad ever caught anyone doing this, his career of picking cotton on the Lee farm was over instantaneously.

For those that do not know, it takes a lot of cotton by volume to equal a pound in weight. The white, puffy balls of cotton are just like those sold in stores except that the cotton in the field has a few small seeds embedded. Picking the cotton from the cotton bolls requires a deft touch and even then, it can be difficult. The cotton can sometimes cling to the boll, as if held in by a small amount of glue. Other times the cotton balls are firm in the boll and have not fluffed up as is normal. When trying to pick this cotton, one would often jab the cotton boll husks that had opened up into the cuticles of the finger nails. As you might imagine, this can be very painful.

In spite of the difficulty in picking large amounts of cotton by weight, some of the people that dad would hire could pick as much as 200 pounds of cotton in a day. These were mostly the older adult men and women who had been picking cotton for many years. They did not waste time with idle chatter in the field nor did they go about their business at a leisurely pace. These were the people who started early in the morning with the hands rapidly going from cotton stalk to sack and back again. Sometimes it was as if these people had about four hands instead of two.

The last year that my dad planted cotton was 1965 or 1966. I was about 12 years old and had finally gotten to the point in cotton picking efficiency that I could pick over 100 pounds in a day. I had reached a milestone. But, I must say that I was not disappointed that my dad decided to quit planting cotton.

About that time, synthetic materials were coming into the marketplace throughout the world, and the price of cotton just wasn't worth the effort to small farmers. I thought this was the reason that we quit growing cotton on the Lee farm. But, I believe that I found out the real reason that my dad quit growing cotton a few days ago, in June of 2005, some 40 years after our last cotton crop.

I had the occasion to be riding with him through the countryside around our home area. We were idly chatting about the return of cotton growing that has taken place during the last few years around our area of the country. It has really made a comeback as an agricultural product for many farmers in our area over the last 10 years or so.

As we were riding along, we began to discuss the growing of cotton and reminisce about those years in the past. I was talking about how hard the work of picking cotton was and how it would be impossible to get people to do that kind of labor today. My dad sort of chuckled and asked me if I knew why he and my Uncle Homer had quit planting cotton. I said that I guessed it was because of the economics of trying to grow it. He said that economics was not the reason. Then he began to confess.

It seems that the last year that cotton was planted on the Lee farm, the crop reached maturity a little later than normal. As stated above, this time was usually just before school started back. This year, the crop reached "pickin' time" just a few days before school started. There was time for the first picking to be completed before all of the kids started school again, but not the second picking. The second picking was going back over the fields again after the cotton had been picked once and gathering all of the cotton that had not matured by the time of the first picking.

Well, the time for the second picking arrived and the only ones left available to do the picking were my dad and my Uncle Homer. My dad told me that they went to the field that day with all intentions of finishing the harvesting of the cotton crop. They worked real hard all day, breaking only for lunch. Late in the afternoon, they weighed the cotton that the two of them had picked together. It weighed less than 100 pounds!! Paying the standard rate of 3 cents a pound, together they would have earned less than $3.00 for the day.

Although they were pretty good growers of cotton, they were not worth anything as pickers. This amount of cotton would be worth about $30.00, maybe a little more at the cotton gin. At the rate they were picking the cotton, it would have taken them about another two weeks, maybe a little less, to complete the task before them. My dad, ever the person of having the ability to put thoughts into concise statements, said he told my Uncle Homer, "Homer, you and me are pretty good at growing cotton but we ain't worth a damn at picking cotton. And, I damn sure ain't fixing to spend my time doing this for the next two weeks. If you want to, you can but I have better things to do."

He left the field that day, went to town the next morning and found a couple of black ladies that he struck a deal with to pick the cotton. If they picked it, he would split the proceeds with them fifty-fifty. They would get half of what the cotton sold for and my dad and Uncle Homer would get the other half.

With that, my dad's cotton picking career was over. So was the planting of cotton on the Lee farm. However it came about, I was not sorry that this was the end of the cotton planting or picking.

A few years ago, I had the occasion to be in the presence of an elderly black man who was working in our school district where I was working as a high school principal. We were talking about times past and somehow the subject of picking cotton came up. He started talking about the job he had at the time, and he said that it was sometimes tough, but not nearly as hard as picking cotton. Then he said, "But, if I get tired of this job, I can go pick cotton again. That is, if I want to. But, I don't believe that I want to do that again."

I have the same exact feeling. Though I have done it before, I hope that I don't have to ever go back and pick cotton again other than to maybe stop by a field, walk to a cotton stalk, and pick a couple of cotton bolls to show my children or grandchildren what it feels like. Other than that, I am a lot like my dad when it comes to picking cotton.

To quote him, "I damn sure don't plan to do that. I have better things to do."

Chapter 10

BUILDING DAMS AND OTHER
ENGINEERING PROJECTS

G rowing up on a farm requires that one obtain a certain amount of knowledge in a wide variety of job skills. Some of these are passed down from one generation to the next by having the children participate in the work that goes on around a farm.

Examples of these skills might include how to plant a garden, how to harvest produce, how to tend to and take care of the various animals on the farm. Other examples might be how to use hand tools like hammers, saws, wrenches, and pliers. These skills might also include being taught how to build a fence, hoe a crop or chop wood.

While the boys were learning the skills named above, the girls were also learning a lot about helping a farm to run successfully. For example, cooking a noontime meal for a bunch of working men required all kinds of abilities. Cleaning vegetables and preparing them for cooking takes a lot of training, for each and every different kind of food requires different preparation skills.

Learning to do laundry, especially in the 1950's and 1960's on our farm also required a lot of training. After all, the clothes that were washed were done in an outside shed on a wringer type washer and hung out on a line to dry. Then, all of the clothes had to be ironed with old fashioned, no steam irons. Wash day on the farm was literally an all day affair that was backbreaking labor for the ladies and young girls. By the way, there was no law against having some of us boys also help with this chore if our hands were idle, especially in drawing and toting the water and emptying the dirty water and refilling the pots. All of these are skills that, if properly learned, can be of tremendous help throughout one's life.

But of all the skills that I learned while growing up on the farm of my parents and grandparents, the one that I really liked to do and one that was a lot of fun was dam building. You just haven't had a full life experience as a child unless you have helped to dam up a small stream on a hot July day, using whatever dam building materials and tools may be available, with nothing on except a pair of cut off jean shorts and maybe a pair of drawers (underwear).

Most of these dam building projects began just like a lot of other activities on the farm. They began with idle time on the hands of young'uns, a suggestion by one of them that it would be fun to build a dam on the creek and a mad rush by all to secure the tools and materials to do the job.

No fancy architectural drawings required! No budget necessary! No blueprints needed! Time was wasting and there was a dam to be built! Watch out snakes, eels, small fish and turtles! A major construction project is coming to your home town creek!

Around our family farm were several suitable sites for dam construction. Depending on how much effort we wanted to exert on any particular day, we could choose any number of options for building a dam. We could do a simple project like damming up the overflow from our farm pond or a much more complex endeavor such as damming up the small stream that crossed the county line dirt road. It was entirely up to the "construction engineers" on which project to tackle.

A typical dam project went something like this. It is about mid-morning in the middle of July and the sun is already scorching hot. It is too hot to work and not a single adult will volunteer to take us to the creek to go swimming. Idle time with nothing to do.

Someone says, "Let's build a dam." That's all it takes. Activity picks up at breakneck speed. A couple of kids grab shovels. A couple of more get the old wheelbarrow from under the shed and begin to hunt anything suitable to use as dam foundation material such as large chunks of concrete and old pieces of fence posts. A couple of more grab 5 gallon buckets to be used as earth movers. Once the preparations are complete, the whole construction company heads down to the chosen spot.

Upon arrival at the area of the creek to be dammed up, all members of the construction crew shucked off clothes down to their cut-off jean shorts. By the way, this was a boy's only activity for the most part. If a girl joined in, she had to have proper attire.

The type of dam to be built depended upon several factors, just as in building a real dam across a large body of water. Several factors had to be considered by the construction company before the commencement of any project. We had to decide how much time we had to complete the project. This was usually from starting time to dinner (lunch) or supper, if it was an afternoon start time. We had to see how wide the body of water was that was to be dammed up. This depended on how much rain we had recently had and on which spot was chosen as the dam site. After all these factors had been taken into account, a quick plan was developed on how this particular dam was to be built and construction began.

We would begin by using any large objects that we had available as foundation pieces, just like any professional dam builder would do. We would place these in the middle of the creek run first, sort of like driving pilings. We would then begin to add other materials to the process such as smaller rocks, pieces of posts, and parts of logs from the surrounding area of the creek. As the flow of the water began to change, we would then begin to add lots of dirt to the dam. Sticks would be embedded for added strength and slowly but surely, the water would begin to back up. On many of these, we would even build fancy spillways around the dam to help take pressure off the main structure.

These dam building projects were valuable learning experiences, too. We learned about the forces of water and how the power of water can damage things. We learned about suitable materials for building projects and which materials are not very good. We learned about adding strength to structures by the interlocking of materials and supplies. Perhaps the most important thing that we learned was that a lot of fun can be had in the middle of a small stream on a hot summer afternoon building a dam.

Some of these were pure works of art! A whole herd of beavers could not have done a better job! Some dams were quite large, two or three feet high and as wide as 20 feet or more. Others were smaller projects, maybe a foot high and less than 10 feet wide. But they all had one thing in common. It was fun building them!!

I am not sure if city kids have the chance to be amateur dam builders or not though I suspect that not many do. They do not know what they have missed. I am glad that this is another experience that I had while being raised in the Bethel Church, county line dirt road community.

Chapter 11

TREASURES OF LIMITED VALUE
AND YET PRICELESS

How do we as human beings determine the value of an item? This is an age old question with no clear answer because people value different things for different reasons. Certainly, some items are of great monetary value while other possessions are worth much less. But, sometimes those items that are of great monetary worth have no real value to the owner, while items of much less monetary worth may be priceless in the eyes of the beholder.

As I considered this question of the ages, it occurred to me that our dearest possessions are often items of little value to anyone else. In essence, these are the belongings that are often a part of our life's foundations and are the things that help us to define who we are as people.

In a "forced field" analysis activity, where one is forced to make decisions about what to do or not do or what to keep or discard, the choices are often very difficult. Activities such as this cause people to carefully consider what their options are because they have to justify their choices to their harshest critics—themselves. There is no one else to help and there is no one else to blame for the choices made. It is just them and their own feelings.

Lists such as these undergo changes during the course of our lives because of many factors. Age, maturity, health, family situations, and many other considerations are just a few of the variables that will cause these changes. I doubt seriously that all of the items that are on my list now, at age 52, would have made my list at age 30, though I am sure that some would have. Given these considerations and the fact that I have given this much thought over the last few months, here is my list of things I would keep if I were forced to choose.

Please understand that the items on this list are all material possessions only. None of these items would ever take the place of my wife, children, grandchildren, parents, or many other loved ones. After all, love is the supreme expression of God's love for us and is our best way of demonstrating this most precious of gifts to others.

With that clearly stated, here goes my list of treasures of limited value and priceless worth. These are not necessarily in order of most to least important. They are all of equal value to me for very different reasons.

The first thing that I have chosen to list is a ring that belonged to my paternal grandfather. This ring that my grandfather, Pa, gave to me when I was about 11 or 12 years old is included because he gave it to me, his baby grandson. He wore this ring for many, many years and owned the ring way before I was born. It is a simple ring made of 10K gold with an engraved image on the side and an "L" on the top of the smooth surface. It was given to him many years ago by a family member, Reverend Bill George, who had bought it. My Pa told him that he really liked it and Bill George gave it to him. He rarely took it off and only then to let me try it on a few times until he gave it to me not long before he died.

He could have given the ring to any number of other grandchildren. They all loved the ring for the same reasons that I do. It belonged to our

Pa, a gentle, kind-hearted man who was loved by all who knew him. But, he gave it to me when my finger finally got big enough for the ring to fit properly. He gave it to me because I was special to him. I knew that then. I know it even more now.

I wore the ring until it became too small for my ring finger. I switched it to my little finger and wore it until my little finger became too large for the ring. My wife had it sized up one time and I continued to wear it until I could no longer get it on. It is now in a jewelry case here at home and will be given to my first grandson, if I ever have one, when he is old enough to understand the meaning that it has to me. It is probably not worth much in terms of money. It is priceless to me.

He also tried to give me his pocket knife, but I would not take it at the time. I told him that he would still need it. I wish I had taken it because upon his death, even though he had promised the knife to me, an aunt took the knife, and I have never seen it again. If I had it, the knife would also be on the list.

Also on my list is a 16-gauge Browning automatic shotgun that my dad bought for me when I was 11 years old. He paid $80.00 for the gun in 1964. It was practically new, having had less than a full box of shotgun shells shot out of it at the time my dad purchased it. He bought it because he wanted me to have the opportunity to develop a love for hunting and the outdoors that he had. This love of his for the outdoors began when he was a boy, and he passed this love on to my brother and me. He bought each of us our own shotgun at about the age of 11 or 12. He made sure that we were properly trained in the use of the weapon and spent hours with us teaching us the proper techniques to safely handle a shotgun. During the next few years, we spent countless hours with our dad going to dove shoots, going quail hunting and deer hunting. Some of the best times of my early teen years were spent in the hunting fields with my dad, brother, and friends involved in the great sport of hunting. From these early experiences, my love of the outdoors and nature took root.

As a person who likes to hunt, I now own several other shotguns and rifles. If I ever have to sell any of them or get rid of them for any reason, all of these others will go first, way before the old Browning. As with the ring, my plan is for it to go on down the line to some family member in the years ahead who will know the story of the shotgun and how special it is to me.

Next on my list is an item that may seem odd to some but not to those that really know me. It is a pitcher, in the shape of "Porky Pig," that belonged to my mother. The old pitcher is made of clay with a por-celain glaze. While I was growing up, my mom used it to make lemonade during the summer. She would also take it on picnics, filled with sweet tea or lemonade, when our family would go to any of the several swim-ming holes up and down Holmes Creek for an afternoon of fun, food, and swimming.

These family picnics would often include one, two, or even three other families in addition to ours. My mom and the other ladies would pack sandwiches, fried chicken, pork and beans, chips, cakes, cookies, and other types of goodies and head to the creek. Often included among the goodies was a homegrown watermelon that we placed in the creek to cool for eating in the afternoon. Upon arrival, all in attendance including dads, moms, and children would swim in the clear, cold water until lunch time. We would then gather around the spread set before us and eat until we could hold no more.

Next came the mandatory hour wait until we could get in the water again. After all, everyone knew back then in the 60's that swimming too quickly after eating would cause cramps and may lead to someone drown-ing. An hour has never passed so slowly as that hour after lunch at the creek in July waiting to go swimming. Most hours are 60 minutes long. That hour after lunch lasted at least 120 minutes, or so it seemed.

Finally, it was time to swim again. Everyone swam for a long while, and then it was time to cut the watermelon. Red, ripe, sweet watermelon juice running down your face, neck and body with not a care in the world is hard to beat. Never mind if the juice did get all over you. It was just going to be washed off in the creek in a few minutes.

The old pig pitcher went with us on many of the outings. It was there on the table often in the summer evenings. After all of us children were grown, gone, and raising families of our own, the pitcher stayed in the china cabinet at my mom and dad's house. Upon my mom's death, my sister, brother, and I removed a few things that meant a lot to us because we did not want them to go missing. I don't know what they took. I got the "Porky Pig" pitcher. I will pass it on to one of my daughters one of these days when the time is right for her to make some lemonade for her children.

Another item that I want to make sure that I have is my mother's Bible. It is an old Bible with pages loose from the binding. It has many dates and times in it that are important to our family. But, the thing I remember the most about this Bible is the beautiful pictures in it that I used to look at as a child. I was looking at it a few months back and it was as if I had traveled through time and was looking at them just like I did when I was much younger. There must be 50 or more of these beautiful pictures, many of them small reproductions of famous artist paintings of Biblical scenes. There are pictures of Moses, Abraham, Jesus, Mary, Peter, and many others. They show the miracles of Jesus, the crossing of the Red Sea and the Ten Commandments being brought down from the Mount Sinai. These images in the pages of God's word are some of my earliest memories of the Bible. Today, the Bible and God's word are the foundation of my life. By the way, I own several other Bibles but this particular Bible, has a special place in my heart.

My wedding band is the last item that I will include on this list. Though my fingers have outgrown the ring, it is still a part of me that would be one of the last things to go if I were forced to make such a choice. It signifies to me the beginning of my life with my wife and all of the wonderful things that have been a part of this relationship for the past 37 years. It signifies the best and worst of times. It includes all of the memories of my children and now my grandchildren. It brings to mind the great friendships that we have developed over the years of our marriage. It causes me to think of the times that we have had to be strong together to meet the challenges of the world that come to all people. Its circle of gold reminds me of the most precious gift that any of us have—that is to unconditionally love and be loved by someone. It is for these reasons that that little ring of gold that is not worth a great deal of money is priceless to me.

As you have read this, I hope it has caused you to reflect on what would be on your own list. What would you include and what would you leave off? Where did they come from? Who gave them to you? Why would certain items be on the list and other items not?

Isn't it sort of strange that in life, we all seem to spend so much of it accumulating things that, in the end, really don't mean much to us and the things that we treasure often come with not much effort on our part?

What is really of little value but priceless to you?

Chapter 12

AMATEUR RODEO ON THE FARM

"Yeeee-haaaww!" "Ride 'em, cowboy!" "Hold on!" "Spur 'em!" Whomp! Thud!

"Daaaadddd-blame! That hurt like the dickens!" Howling laughter erupts from all those in attendance that are sitting on the fence surrounding the "arena." "All right! Who's next?"

Thus usually went the flow of action at any of the many amateur rodeos that took place on the Lee family farm while I was growing up. These amateur rodeo events were just one of the countless types of self-entertainment that my brother, our cousins, friends and I participated in while growing up on the farm that my grandfather homesteaded in the early 1900's in southern Holmes County, just north of the Washington County line. And, I must confess, these wild-west shows were often better than the Northwest Florida Championship Rodeo that was, and still is, held in my hometown of Bonifay, Florida every October.

These down-on-the-farm rodeos had all of the excitement of the real ones uptown. However, these events were really more like the bull riding event than the entire rodeo. This was because most of the time, the only rough stock that we had to ride were the half-grown calves from our herd of beef cattle, plus the occasional calf of one of the milk cows that my brother and I milked every morning before school. At these rodeos, we also had an ample supply of clowns, though none of them had the fancy make-up or wild costumes.

For those who know little about rodeos, please allow me to explain some of the requirements that help any rodeo to be successful. First, every decent rodeo has to have a promoter, a person that makes sure that all necessary items are taken care of for the show to go on.

This job always went to my older brother, Silas. For you see, Silas has been a cowboy since the first day he drew a breath of air on the earth. I am pretty sure that his first pair of baby shoes was a pair of Red Rider cowboy boots complete with high heels, sharp toes and spurs. If not his first pair, then for sure his second pair. He ain't never wore no regular shoes unless he was made to wear some to church while growing up. (Notice the use of proper cowboy talk.)

He is a person that has always loved fooling with cows and horses. He loved to ride horses growing up and still loves it today at age 54. This love of horses started early. According to my sister, when he was just a toddler, he would fall asleep while riding a red, wooden bouncy horse pretending to be a cowboy. He loved to be around cowboys. He practiced roping and riding. To practice the roping, he would try to lasso anything that was standing still or moving including stumps, fence posts, calves and me. To practice riding, he built contraptions out of ropes and 55 gallon drums to simulate bull and bareback riding. It is a wonder that some of us were not seriously injured or killed on these marvelous feats of engineering designed to simulate the movements of a bucking horse or bull.

He rode rough stock (bulls mostly) in real rodeos when he reached the age to do so until a bull dang near tore his leg off one night in Pensacola, Florida. As a matter of fact, my dad told him something one time that clearly demonstrates his love for cows. When Silas was a teenager, my dad told him, and I quote, "Son, you are the only teenage boy I know that would rather smell cow s_ _t than perfume." Nuff said about my brother and his love for cows.

In his role as the promoter, it was his job to direct the gathering up of the stock to be used in that particular rodeo, make sure that there were enough "cowboys" entered in the event, and to see to it that there was a crowd of folks around to watch the entertainment. Since we always had a small herd of cattle on the farm and plenty of willing cousins to be the "cowboys" and the spectators, he fulfilled these responsibilities with a high degree of professionalism.

Second, every rodeo has to have a rough stock contractor, one that provides all of the animals that are to be used in a rodeo for the contestants to ride. Well shoot, this job was also taken, so to speak. This position was filled by my dad. After all, it was his cows that had the calves that we penned up and tried our best to ride.

Though most contractors are paid a large sum of money for furnishing the stock to a rodeo, the opposite was true for my dad. It cost him lots of money to feed and clothe Silas, my older sister Janis and me. It also costs a ton of money to maintain a herd of beef cattle including but surely not limited to pasture lands, hay, and winter grazing. So, instead of making money for being the stock contractor, my dad was losing money on the deal every day.

Third, you need a group of cowboys that are willing to pay the price to ride or the entry fee. Now, at a real rodeo, these entry fees are paid in the form of money. At our rodeos, the only entry fee required to be a cowboy was to be just crazy enough to climb on. For a bunch of pre-teen to early teen aged boys raised on the farm, this included just about everybody.

At real rodeos, cowboys use very expensive equipment to help them complete their rides and make the whistle. These include fancy riding ropes for bulls, saddles and bridles for saddle bronco horses, and "riggings" for riding bareback horses. Cowboys have these made especially for them and they carry them from rodeo to rodeo in special cases and storage containers. My brother tells me that a man's riding rig is the most important tool that he has in his possession as a rodeo cowboy.

At our rodeos, we also had real fancy riding rigs. These often consisted of a single strand of hay bailing twine or any old piece of rotten rope that we could find that would fit around a calf. If we really were trying to look "official", we might plait 3 pieces of bailing twine together so that it would be a tad stronger for some of that really rough stock that we rode. As might be guessed, there were many times that a broke rigging was the cause of the elegant dismounts that we routinely made. (In case you have forgotten, see paragraph one!)

Last, but not least, every rough stock contractor wants to bring the best bucking stock he has to the rodeo. Well, we were always able to find a half-grown, Hereford calf or two that was perfectly willing to do their best to fill this very important role. They were absolutely wild, definitely committed to getting us off their back and most of the time, more than capable of getting it done in just a couple of jumps out of the shoot. The cowboy that reached the 8-second count on one of these was usually the winner of the rodeo, hands down.

At one of these rodeos, I was the featured cowboy or at least I was until that calf threw me and broke my collarbone. My brother, ever the compassionate person, as most older siblings are, came to my aid. By the way, I was just a little over 6-years old when this happened.

Did I say my brother came to my aid? Well, he did, sort of. He did see that I was in pain and hurting. (Again, see paragraph one for explanation.) He did come over to me. With the utmost amount of compassion for me, he told me that I should not tell mom and dad what had happened because they might get mad at us for riding calves. He convinced me that the injury was not real bad and that the pain would go away in a little while. Being the younger brother, I went along. I surely did not want mom and dad to be mad at us.

After about two days of hurting and trying my best to hide the pain from my parents, my mom, who was a nurse, noticed that I was favoring my arm. I could barely lift it over my head to put on a tee shirt without severe pain. After observing this a couple of times, she asked me what was wrong with my shoulder. In spite of my concern about getting in trouble, I fessed up about what had happened and when it had happened.

She immediately took me to the doctor for x-rays. Sure enough, I had a broken collar bone. To this day, this is the only broken bone that I have ever had except for the broken nose received in football practice as a junior in high school, courtesy of an elbow through the facemask.

My mom and dad scolded my brother and me a little about not telling them the truth. They were, as you would expect, more upset about us not telling than about riding the calves. To the best of my memory, the only punishment either of us got was a severe tongue lashing. Also, as best as I can recall, this was the most severe injury that ever happened at any of these rodeos. This is probably a great example of the Lord watching over and taking care of idiots, both old and young.

Did this little tragedy end the amateur rodeos? Not hardly! Just as soon as I was healed up enough to participate again, I was right back in the game. After all, a little idle time and nothing better to do is a great reason to have a rodeo!

Yeeee-hawaa!" "Ride 'em, boy!" "Hold on!" "Spur 'em!" Whomp! Thud! "Daaaadddd-blame! That hurt like the dickens!"

The rodeo is back in town.

Chapter 13

BROTHERS, BICYCLES AND KNIVES

The first bicycle that my brother, Silas, and I had was a used one that my dad obtained from some acquaintance of his and brought home. It was an older bicycle with large tires, no chrome in sight, and a second hand paint job of solid black. To say the least, it was not a shiny, new store-bought model that was available uptown at either Ingram's Western Auto store or at Bowen Hardware. But, used or not, shine or no shine, whatever the color, it served the purpose - we had a bicycle to ride!

For the most part, we shared the one bicycle without a whole lot of problems other than the normal arguments between brothers as to whose turn it was to ride the bike. There were also a few finger pointing incidents between us blaming one another for leaving the bicycle out in the weather after we had finished riding it for the day instead of making sure it was put under the barn or well shed to keep it dry and to help prevent it from rusting.

That old bicycle was the only ride in town for the two of us and we generally took pretty good care of it. As we were familiar with the tools used to work on farm equipment, we became pretty good at fixing any mechanical problems which the bicycle had. We could oil the chain, air up the tires, put the chain back on if it slipped off and adjust the seat height. We could even adjust the spokes on the tires to keep the wheels properly aligned. We could also change an inner tube in the tires and remount the wheels on the front and back.

While we were doing this mechanic work on the old bicycle, we would use some of dad's tools. And, like most kids, we would often leave the wrench, pliers, screw driver or oil can sitting right where we were working on the bike, forgetting to put these tools in their proper place. Sometimes the tools would lay there for a couple of hours if we happened to remember to put them up or sometimes they might stay right there several days.

Either way, when dad would happen by and see these tools left out, he would speak to us in a manner that did not require a lot of interpretation to understand what he was saying or what he meant. Today, the manner in which he spoke to us would be considered harsh though I can't tell that being spoken to in a harsh manner back then has had any lasting negative impact on the psychological health of either my brother or me.

When he would discover some of his tools that had been left out, he would search one of us out and the conversation would generally go something like this. "Boy, how many times am I going to have to tell you and your brother to put them damn tools up when you finishing using them. Now, get your ass out there to that barn and put them up right now!" As a result of these conversations with dad, I must have been 11 or 12 years old before I even knew that the word tools was just one word. Up until then, I thought "damn tools" was all together like a compound word. Anyway, these teachings of dad about his tools eventually took with me as I am very ill if someone uses some of my tools today and does not return them to their proper place.

Getting back to the bicycle, as I said, generally Silas and I shared the bicycle without a lot of problems. But, on one particular day, we did have a little disagreement about whose turn it was to ride. In this instance, it seemed to me that Silas had been taking more than his share of the riding time on this day. I had asked several times for him to let me ride but he kept on riding.

Finally, out of frustration, when he came by me one time, I gave him a hard shove, causing him to lose his balance and wreck. This wreck caused a couple of skinned knees, maybe a scrape or two here and there and one really ill, older brother. As soon as he got up, he came after me seeking retribution.

Like any younger, smaller brother, I took off to avoid the pending butt kicking. However, I made a serious miscalculation. Instead of running toward the house, where there were some adults who could have interceded in the situation, for some reason I took off running up the road and away from home. As the chase progressed, it became obvious to me that Silas was going to catch me and I was going to get the worst end of the deal.

So, without a real understanding of the consequences of what I was about to do, I wheeled around, reached down to my side and whipped out my trusty hunting knife. I pulled a knife on my brother!!

Now truth be told, this knife was probably not real dangerous to my brother. I had bought it a few days before at the Western Auto for the price of $1.00. It came complete with a plastic handle and a fake leather scabbard. It looked like a small version of the one Daniel Boone carried every week on television. The blade was made of metal but to sharpen it would have required a lot of time and effort. In other words, it was so dull that it wouldn't cut butter, much less someone. But, it did have a sharp point and looked dangerous.

When I pulled the knife, my brother stopped in his tracks as I was wildly swinging it back and forth in a desperate demonstration of survival 101. When he saw the knife, his only comment was "I'm going to tell Dad." and he headed back to the house.

When dad got home that afternoon, my brother was true to his word. He did indeed tell my dad that I had pulled a knife on him. Even though dad listened to the whole story about the incident beginning with me shoving Silas off the bike for not sharing the ride, he still took corrective action about me pulling the knife. In other words, he whipped my butt for doing something so dangerous. He also gave me a strong lecture about the proper uses of a knife and took my knife away from me for a period of time. Since that day, I have never had the desire to pull a knife on anyone again.

The old bicycle finally wore out and we could no longer fix it up and keep it going. The next Christmas, I got a shiny new bicycle complete with a small book rack on the back and double headlights powered by two "D" batteries. It was a brand new, store bought Western Flyer straight from the hardware store. I was once again mobile and ready to roam around the roads close to home.

I am sure that my brother also rode this bike. I am pretty sure that we argued occasionally about whose turn it was to ride, though I do not remember for sure. I do know for a fact that I never was tempted to pull a knife on him again over this or anything else. I learned that lesson real good with just one short instructional period from dad.

Chapter 14

FIRECRACKER IN THE HAND!

I can remember a time during my childhood when it was common for children to have fireworks at special times of the year, particularly around the 4th of July and during the Christmas holiday season. This was way before everyone in the world became so aware of the dangers of fireworks around children and passed laws to protect us from ourselves.

We always looked forward to these times when my parents and other parents in our neighborhood would buy these fireworks and would allow us to have the pleasure of playing with them. As a side thought, what is it about hearing the loud "pop" of a firecracker or "cherry bomb" that is so entertaining? This is a question that can't be answered in this short essay. Anyway, the times when we were allowed to have these fireworks were always looked forward to with anticipation and excitement.

As I recall, there were many different types of fireworks that were present. There were the regular firecrackers that made a loud "bang". There were the "cherry bombs" that were red in color, like small round balls that were more powerful than regular firecrackers. Then, there were some things called M-80's that were even more powerful than "cherry bombs." There were also many other types of fireworks such as Roman Candles that shot exploding fireworks into the air, bottle rockets that would fly through the air before exploding, sparklers that gave off brilliant amounts of light and little miniature firecrackers called "lady fingers" that were about ¼ the size of regular firecrackers. These "lady fingers" would work only about half of the time or so it seemed. This was the reason that some people did not give them the proper respect that was due any firework. More on this later.

We always had a lot of fun during these times. We would put firecrackers under tin cans and watch them blow up into the air. We would see how far a bottle rocket would go before it exploded. We would watch the Roman Candles shoot the fireworks high into the air before exploding. Especially entertaining was watching what a "cherry bomb" or "M-80" could do to a syrup can or to a small cardboard box when it exploded. By the way, parents were always around when these larger types of fireworks were used, so they had not completely lost their minds and turned us foot loose and fancy free.

One of the favorite things for the older kids to do was to light the firecrackers while holding them and tossing them out into the air. Even though in retrospect this was dangerous, at the time we did not see it that way. We were just having fun.

One night, my brother and I, along with several other friends and cousins, were playing with these fireworks. We had run out of everything but some firecrackers and we were lighting them and throwing them. However, the firecrackers that we had left were "Blackcat" brand firecrackers, the undisputed best brand of firecrackers in the world, at least as determined by those of us who lived in the Bethel Church / county line dirt road community. No other kind of firecracker was a good as a "Blackcat."

Now when you are throwing firecrackers, you must always be aware of two factors that determine how fast a firecracker fuse burns. First is its length and second is how much powder is on the fuse. The most important of these two factors is the length of the fuse. After all, a short fuse means a short time to get rid of the firecracker after it has been lit. But, it is also important to be aware if the fuse is covered with powder as this will cause the fuse to burn faster. When a firecracker had a short fuse with powder on it, you were well advised to just lay it on the ground and watch it explode.

However, you could not always tell if a fuse had a lot of powder on it and sometimes the fuse burned real quickly, giving the holder not much time to rid himself of the firecracker. Once in a great while, one would go off just after leaving the hand. On this particular night, one went off in my hand just before I let it go.

When it popped, it felt like my fingers had been blown off. Luckily there was not any damage at all other than it hurt like hell! I began to cry and was headed inside to show my mom and dad when my ever compassionate, older brother spoke up. He said, "Don't go inside and tell them! If you do, they won't let us play with the firecrackers anymore!" This was a classic example of not letting a little pain (A lot of pain!) for someone else get in the way of more fun for others. He tried his best to keep me from my appointed duties of letting my mother, the nurse, attend to my injuries.

This time, I did not let him prevail. I took off to the front door and went into the house. I went directly to my mom and told her what had happened. To this point in time, I apparently had not even looked at my hand because when she told me that all my fingers were still on my hand, my response between sniffles was, "See, all my fingers *are* still there!" My mom and dad told that story to many people over the next few years.

Getting back to the fact that we did not give fireworks the respect due them, I suppose that this incident certainly qualifies. However, I know of another case where a friend of mine showed his lack of respect in a situation that involved the little "lady finger" firecrackers. As I said earlier, these "lady finger" were notorious for not working. In some cases it seemed that only about 1 out of 5 would "pop" as they were supposed to do.

So, kids being kids, some with a little sense and some with not quite as much, we were playing with the "lady fingers" one day, lighting them and throwing them. One of the boys who was with us by the name of Donald, decided that they weren't working anyway and he would be brave and hold one in his lips. Did I say that some kids don't have any sense?

As luck, in this case bad luck, would have it, this particular "lady finger" worked just fine. When it went off in that kid's lips, the look on his face was, as they say in the television advertisement, priceless. Luckily, the only lasting damage from this incident was a bloody lip and some ringing ears. It did not loosen any teeth nor do any other type of permanent damage. However, it did convince Donald not to take chances with fireworks anymore, even "lady fingers." If made a believer out of him and the others of us who witnessed this incident.

In looking back on these times, I now realize how dangerous it was for us to play with these firecrackers and other types of fireworks mostly unsupervised by adults. I don't let my children play with fireworks unless I am watching closely because of the dangers involved. But, for those of us who grew up during the times when we could do this, it was a lot of fun and provided us with lasting memories of good times with family and friends.

Chapter 15

⸺⸻⸺

DOLLY AND MOLLY, SILAS AND ME

Early each morning for several years, my brother Silas and I had standing dates with two old gals who lived on our farm. These gals were always at the same place anxiously awaiting our arrival. They were always glad to see us and would call for us in loud voices if we were late for our dates. These dates were set for each and every day, weekends included, rain or shine, cold or hot, spring summer, fall, and winter.

During these morning dates, we always fed the girls a good meal, spent some up close time with them, talked with them and even rubbed on them a little bit. These girls were named Dolly and Molly and though they had similar names, they were no kin to each other.

You see, the dates that my brother and I had each morning were with our two milk cows who supplied all of the milk that was consumed by our family and a couple of other families in the neighborhood. It was one of those chores that had to be done each and every morning on the farm and my dad delegated this chore to us two growing boys. This chore was another of those that was not a lot of fun as it required not only the actual act of milking the cows each morning but also a good bit of work in preparation for the milking.

Milking the two cows each morning actually started the afternoon before when the cows and their calves had to be located and penned up for the night. This made it necessary to locate and get the cows and calves into the barn each day, separating the cows from the calves, and then feeding and watering each pair of animals.

Of course, locating and getting the animals into the barn each afternoon could turn into an adventure unto itself. On some days, the cows would be standing right outside of the barn yard just waiting to be let in. On these days, it was a simple task, taking little time and effort to get the animals into the barn, fed and watered for the night.

On some other days, the chore was not as easy as described above but still, not too difficult. On these days, the cows might be a little ways away but still within sight of the barn. You could maybe give them a call that we learned from our dad or Uncle Homer and the cows would often respond and head toward the barn. Or, if they did not respond, we could make a short trip into the field and drive them to the barn using some hay or corn as enticements for them to make the trip.

But on some other days, it was an adventure. On these days, the cows would be just as far away from the barn as they could get in the 80 acres or so that was contained in their feeding grounds. They would not respond to any manner of calling that we did in an effort to get them to the barn. On these days, we would have to walk however far it was to try and drive them toward the desired location. Sometimes, they would go right toward the barn with no further problems. However, on some days, they would not go at all. They would want to go back to where they were grazing or maybe circle around you and head back to another part of the pasture. Or, they might just head out into the pond for a drink of water before heading toward the barn, leaving you standing on the hill. Sometimes these adventures would take 30 minutes or more before the cows and calves would be safely in the barn for the night.

Now I know that what I am going to say is probably just my memory playing tricks on me but danged if it didn't seem back then that the easy days of getting those cows into the pin happened on the days when the sun was shining bright with clear blue skies and pleasant temperatures. On the days when it was an adventure, it seemed that this always happened on a day when it was raining or cold or when you had someplace you needed to be in a hurry or on a day when football practice had lasted longer than normal and it was getting dark outside.

Anyway, by whatever means necessary and however long it took each afternoon, the cows and calves had to be placed in the barn, watered and fed.

When the morning came, it was time to do the milking. As I said earlier, the two cows that we had and milked the longest were Dolly and Molly. These were two Jersey dairy cows that gave large quantities of milk each day. Silas milked Dolly and I milked Molly. Dolly would produce over 10 quarts of milk each morning from only three teats. Molly would also produce almost this amount of milk each morning. (We saved the last teat each morning for the calf.) If you are counting, that is about 20 quarts or five gallons of milk each day which is why we could supply not only the needs of our family, but the needs of others in the neighborhood as well.

While Dolly would produce a little more milk each morning in volume, Molly's milk was much richer in butter fat content. Her milk would yield about two or three inches of pure cream on the top of a 10 quart milk bucket each morning. Because of this, we were never short of real cream for whipping, making our own butter, or for pouring over fresh fruits such as strawberries and peaches.

When milking a cow, one must make sure they are prepared for the chore in every way each morning. For example, if it is raining, you need to make sure that your rubber boots are handy. Trust me, you really do not want to venture into a wet and nasty barnyard early in the morning with your brand new Converse tennis shoes on your feet. They may never be white again!! They will also leave ugly tracks on the kitchen floor when you return to the house which has been known to cause certain females living in the house to have strong and lasting hydraulic fits. (Hydraulic fit – an act of emotional displeasure just short of a nuclear meltdown.)

You must also be prepared to properly clean the utter and teats of the cow each morning. Again, you really do not want to be grabbing hold of some things that a cow may choose to sleep in during the night in a barn-yard. Without proper cleansing, you might just be left "holding the bag" if you get my drift.

As the cows have to be fed in a trough located in the milking area, you have limited choices as to where to set your milking stool each morning. Therefore, you should also be prepared to remove certain amounts of "yesterday's grass" from the immediate area of where you need to locate your milking stool by having a shovel at hand. Otherwise, you may once again encounter certain odors and stains that can add to the experience of milking a cow.

Once the milking had been completed each morning, we would take the milk into our house where my mother would strain the milk through a fine linen cloth to get out any foreign materials that may have gotten into the milk during the milking process. She would then divide the milk into glass gallon jugs that would be distributed to those who would be getting the milk that day.

With a family of five, two growing boys, and a couple of farm hands eat-ing on most days, our family would consume a gallon of milk almost every day. This milk was not pasteurized, homogenized, skimmed, or 2% milk. This was the pure stuff complete with all of the butter fat and cream that is removed from most store bought milk today. I remember when I first started drinking store bought milk that it tasted like water had been added after drinking pure, whole milk for all of those years growing up.

Chapter 16

I'LL HAVE SOME DYNAMITE, DDT AND A LITTLE DAB OF MERCURY

My brother, sister and I rarely get the chance to just visit with one another for any length of time because of the busy lives we all lead. However, a few days ago, one of these opportunities came as we were traveling together for a few hours going to and returning from the funeral of a relative. As we proceeded on our journey, we discussed many topics such as relatives and family connections, our parents (both of whom are deceased), and memories of our childhood years on the family farm.

One of the many topics we discussed during this time together was the fact that we had somehow survived at all considering how many dangerous things we had been exposed to during childhood. We survived riding in cars with no seat belts, traveled regularly in the back of pick-up trucks traveling at high rates of speed, and drank water from a dug well with no chlorine in it but plenty of frogs and other creatures swimming around in the water. We also drank raw, whole milk, with the only purification before being consumed was it had been strained through a cheese cloth to remove all the impurities that may have fallen into the milk while it was being obtained from Molly and Dolly, our two milk cows.

While these exposures to possible danger may have presented ample opportunities for injury or negative health consequences, they can't even begin to compare with some of the very real dangers that were present on the farm and to which we were exposed. In looking back, I don't know if we were just dang lucky or if it was by the grace of God that all of us lived after being exposed to some of these.

One of the dangers to which we were exposed on a regular basis was DDT or dichlorodiphenyltrichloroethane. As is now well known, DDT was an insecticide that was found to be a carcinogen to humans. It also was the cause of many environmental concerns, particularly the effects of large amounts being released into the environment without understanding the long term consequences. In fact, a book titled "Silent Spring" by American biologist Rachel Carson, which was published in 1962, detailed the environmental damages caused by the widespread use of DDT and was one of the events that launched the environmental movement in the United States and the world.

However, at the time we were being raised on the Lee family farm, we used DDT on a regular basis to help control insects in our gardens and around home. It was a common practice for my dad or Uncle Homer to liberally dust garden plants such as tomatoes, beans, peas, okra, and squash with DDT early in the morning while the dew was still on the plants so the DDT would stick to the leaves and kill the insects that may have been feeding on the plants. It dang sure worked, too! DDT would kill tomato worms, cut worms, and any other insect that was attacking our garden.

DDT was also sprinkled around the entrances to barns, feed storage rooms, the corn crib, and even the house to help keep out or kill ants, roaches, spiders, and flies. As in the garden, it worked real well for these purposes also.

All of us kids and the adults handled DDT like we handled many other products at the time. It was just one of the things we used on the farm and we took very few precautions when using the product. In fact, when DDT was banned from use, it was common for many of the folks who lived around us, our family included, to go to the local feed and seed stores and buy up a good supply of the available DDT to have for future use, paying little or no attention to the dangers that were being talked about by governmental types.

As a further explanation of how common our exposure to DDT was as children, I must relate this story. While growing up, there was an old car that all of us kids called "The Jigger" out under one of our barns. This old car did not run anymore and in fact, was just a part of the body of a car with no motor. The back of the car had been cut away and it was just the shell of a 1940's automobile. It did not even have a front seat. But, it did have a steering wheel and a gear lever on the column and all of us "drove" the old car on trips to who knows where in our imagination and pretend games of childhood. And while the car did not have a front seat for these trips, there were often items in the front of the car on which we sat as we pretended to drive the old "Jigger".

One of the items that served as a seat for the driver on these imaginary trips was --- a large bag or sack containing DDT. This sack was not a small one but rather a bag that probably contained 50 pounds of DDT when new. The front of the old car was the perfect storage spot as it was dry, convenient and easy to reach when a little of the product was needed. It also served as a great seat for driving the old Jigger. My how times have changed!!!!

Knowing what we know now about DDT, I guess we are very lucky that none of us have suffered any negative health affects as a result of exposure to this dangerous product.

Another dangerous product that I was exposed to as a child, as hard as this may be to believe in today's world, was liquid mercury. As almost everyone knows today, exposure to mercury is highly dangerous and can lead to many health problems including cancer. The time that I can remember being exposed to mercury actually happened because I had been good. It happened like this.

As a child, Bonifay did not have a dentist in town for a few years, so my mother would take me over to another nearby town, DeFuniak Springs, Florida, to have dental work done. The dentist was a Dr. Sheehee and as I recall, he was a pretty good dentist. On this particular day, I was a very good patient for a young kid, allowing him to complete his work without acting out. As a reward for this good behavior, he gave me one of the little paper cups that was used to sip water out of and expectorate into the little sink by the chair back then (boy was that a long time ago) with a small amount of the liquid mercury in the cup.

The amount he gave me was about the size of a dime, maybe a little less. It was very heavy for such a small amount and had the consistency of something like Jell-O but more slippery. It would stick together and could be rolled around the bottom of the cup without breaking apart. Dr. Sheehee even showed me how he could turn a penny into silver by using a small amount of the mercury to color the penny. I was amazed at this and could not wait to get home and show this trick to my brother and sister.

I played with the mercury all the way home and used it to color several pennies upon arrival. To a little boy of about 8, this was a pretty cool reward for being good at the dentist.

My how times have changed!! About 25 years later, while serving as the principal at a high school, we discovered that we had some liquid mercury stored in our chemistry laboratory. We were required to take special precautions in handling the mercury and had to use hazardous materials disposal rules to even get it removed from the school. I say again, my how times have changed!!

And, without a doubt, the most dangerous item to which we had access while growing up was one that would not cause long term problems, like the DDT or mercury, but was one that could have had immediate and deadly consequences. This product was ----- dynamite!!!

Yep, that's right - D-Y-N-A-M-I-T-E!!! As in BOOOOM!!, you're dead!!!

This dynamite was stored on a shelf in one of our barns within easy reach of anyone who ventured into the room in which it was stored. The shelf was about waist high and the dynamite was stored in its original, wooden box with a lid on it with the word "Dynamite" printed on the side along with the words "Dangerous" and Explosives". This dynamite was just like you may have seen on television, sticks about 1" in diameter and about 12" long, wrapped in red paper.

The fuse cord and caps were also stored in this same room but in a different area on a shelf that was a little harder to reach but still accessible if one was determined to do so.

The reason the dynamite was present was simple. My dad was licensed to use the dynamite on the farm. He would use it to blast stumps out of the ground when clearing land for farm purposes. To do this, he would use about ¼ of a stick of dynamite stuck down into a hole that had been dug out on one side of the stump. He would light the fuse, run and get behind a tree or maybe his truck, and wait for the blast. Believe me, when that dynamite went off, the stump was coming out of the ground.

He would also use a small amount of the explosive to blow these stumps apart once out of the ground. Large stumps can weight upwards of 500 pounds so breaking them down into smaller pieces was impor-tant. He would do this by drilling a hole in the stump and inserting a small piece of dynamite into the hole, lighting it and then standing back a good way, and watching it split the stump apart. Blasting the stumps into smaller, easier to handle pieces allowed us to then complete the pro-cess of cutting these stumps into usable pieces with saws and axes for the fireplace at home or to provide heat for cooking of cane syrup that was done every year in the late fall.

Now, I must point out that my dad had spoken to every one of us children about the dangers of this dynamite and we all knew better than to mess with it. However, children are children and it is a wonder that some of us did not let curiosity get the better of us when we were out in the shop working on a bike or repairing some other toy when no adult was around to tell us no.

After I was an adult and had been away from home for several years, I was out in the shop one day just looking around while visiting my parents. To my surprise, the box of dynamite was still there. I almost fainted when I saw it! I carefully looked at the box without touching it. I then went into the house and asked my dad if he knew the dynamite was still in the barn. His response was, "Why hell yeah, I know it's there!! It is right where it has been." I told him that it was very dangerous to still have as it was likely unstable after all these years and probably needed to be destroyed. He made some response to this suggestion in the line of he would take care of it. A few months later, he did in fact have someone remove the dynamite and explode it harmlessly on the back 40 of our farm. It is probably really fortunate that there was not some accident with this dynamite years earlier.

Though dynamite, DDT, and mercury were not the only dangers to which we were exposed as children, thankfully we did not suffer any long or short term consequences from these exposures. A few years from now, someone else will probably look back and discuss their exposure to some unknown dangers of today that are discovered. Whoever that may be, I hope they are as lucky as we were.

I guess we ought to get some T-shirts that say "I Survived Growing Up On The Lee Family Farm".

Chapter 17

GETTING TO SCHOOL WAS
AN ADVENTURE

A few years back, the U.S. Army had an advertising campaign that included the line, "It's not just a job. It's an adventure!" With just slight modification, this describes the morning ritual of my mother, sister, brother and me trying to get out of the house and getting to school every morning.

My mother was supposed to be at work at 8:00 each morning. Since we lived about five miles outside of town, we needed to leave each morning at about 7:45 a.m. to have time for her to take me to the elementary school and my brother and sister to the high school and get to work on time. But, we never, and I mean never, left for school earlier than about five minutes until 8:00. Most days, we would not get out of the house and into the old Mercury until 8:00 or even 8:05 which made us late daily.

Each day the routine was pretty much the same and it seems as if we could have solved this problem without much effort. But, every day, we would leave later than we should have and would end up being late to school which also resulted in my mother being late to work.

Each day, my mother would start getting us up about 6:15 a.m. Just because she woke us up did not mean we immediately got up. We would lie around a few minutes, wasting time, until she could get us out of bed and moving about. She would begin to cook breakfast for us while my brother and I would go milk cows.

This chore was a daily must and this was one of the factors that led to us being late each day. The reason this was a factor was because my brother was the all time champion of "assling around" which was my mother's expression for wasting time or dragging one's feet. I am pretty sure the word "assle" (from which the word *assling* would come) is not even in the dictionary. But, I do know for sure that it was in my mother's vocabulary and was used regularly as directed toward my brother almost every morning when he would be wasting time before we headed to the barn to milk the cows.

Often, I would already be at the barn and milking before my brother would even make it to the cow pen to begin milking his cow. Once the milking was done, the milk still had to be strained, placed into glass jugs, and put into the refrigerator before the chore was complete. Many times, I would be back in the house, eat my breakfast, brush my teeth, and put on my school clothes while my brother was still at the barn milking or, as my mom would say, assling around. In fact, on more than one occasion, my mother, sister, and I would be headed out of the house to get in the car or already be in the car when my brother would just be coming back into the house from milking. It was on these days when my mother would really let my brother have it for "assling around" and making us late.

My sister would do whatever girls do to get ready to go anywhere. In other words, while my brother and I were doing the milking chore, my sister would be in the one bathroom we had primping, putting on her make-up, and re-doing her hair about three or four times to get it just right. The fact that we had only one bathroom was also a factor in our being late. Having four people trying to use one restroom in the morning to get ready was always an issue. My sister could take hours in the restroom, or so it seemed. My mom also had to have her time for make-up and hair. Throw in the allotted time for my brother and me, and the one restroom was a busy place every morning.

Once we would all finally be ready and in the car, the adventure of the trip itself would begin. As I said, we lived about five miles, as the crow flies, from town. But, the dirt roads that led from our house to town didn't go as the crow flies, and the commute to town took about ten minutes. The road that we took to town most days was known as the "County Line" road as it was on the border between Holmes and Washington counties. This was a dirt road with all of the dust, ruts, bumps, and humps that one would imagine on a dirt road.

When it was rainy weather, this road would become very slippery, and on more than one occasion, we ended up in the ditch while going to school. When it was dry and hot, the dust would swallow up our vehicle as we traveled along. At that time, my mom's car was not air conditioned, so we would ride with the windows down during warm weather and the old car would just fill up with all of that dust.

As a side note to this, I feel I must add one short story about my sister Janis here. When she got old enough to get her driver's license, she would let my brother Silas and me ride with her sometimes. Once while we were riding along in the heat of the summer, she made us roll up the windows in my mom's car. She told us she was doing this to make folks who saw us think we had air-conditioning in the car. She didn't want folks to see us and think we were poor folks that could not afford air-conditioning! Just a tad on the vain side for one that was poor, raised in the country, and who didn't have a sign of any air-conditioning in that dang hot car!

Anyway, as we were late most every morning, my mom would be flying down this road at a high rate of speed, trying her best to be no later than we already were. We used to say that our tires only touched the road on the hilltops during these morning runs. If we happened to meet someone else on the road during one of these trips, we would hold on for dear life as we would pass the other vehicle, leaving them in a cloud of dust as we proceeded on our way. I am sure some of these people we met on the dirt road each morning came to recognize my mom's car and knew to get the heck out of the way of that crazy woman driving like A. J Foyt on a one-lane dirt road.

When we would arrive at school, depending upon how late we were, my sister and brother would have to get tardy slips because they were in high school. I would just go on to class at the elementary school. After a few times of being late at the beginning of each year, my sister's teachers would stop making her get the slips because she was a straight "A" student and would tell them it was her brother's fault she was late. But, my brother, having this same habit of "assling around" at school as well as at home, would even be later than my sister. So almost every day he would have to go to the office, get a tardy slip, and sometimes even have a visit with the principal for a little encouragement to arrive on time. One time the principal even asked my brother why he was late every single day when Janis was never late even though they rode the same car to school—not knowing that she was late too but just had a teacher who did not send her to the office for the tardy slip.

About the time my sister graduated from high school, the county finally paved a road pretty close to our home. So, instead of taking the county line road each morning, we began to use this paved road for our morning trips to school. It was on this road one morning that a funny thing happened about getting to school.

As usual, we were late as we headed to school. Just because the road was paved did not mean our habits of being late changed. My brother was still "assling around" each morning, and we would head out on our adventure of getting to school. Really, about the only thing that changed was that on the paved road my mom could go even faster as she tried to make up the time for being late.

On this particular morning, my mother was just flying as we headed to town. I was riding in the front seat, and my brother was in the back seat. The road we were traveling on had a fairly sharp curve with limited visibility around it. We were going about 60 miles an hour around this corner when all of a sudden, up ahead, a pick-up truck, with galvanized pipes sticking out the back of the bed, was *backing* down this road on the blind curve.

My mom screamed, slammed on the brakes, and finally brought the car to a stop. By the time we got stopped, we were right behind the truck. My mom was shaken up at the thought of how close we came to having a major accident. About this time, things began to get interesting (and funny).

The man who was driving the truck got out and walked back towards the car. Though he could not hear her at this time, my mom was saying a few choice words about the man. As he got closer, my mom reached over me and at a very rapid rate, rolled the window down so she *could talk to the man where he could hear* her. As he approached the car, my mom lit into him about how stupid he was to be backing down the road on a curve with pipes sticking out the back of his truck. Among several of the things she said during this time was, "Mister, just what in the hell do you think you are doing, backing down this road on a curve?"

Listening to this really angry woman talking harshly to him and looking around for any type of relief he could find, the man thought he had discovered a small fact that might just help his cause a little. He said to my mom while pointing to a sign just ahead of his truck, "Lady, just look at that sign. The speed limit here is only 40 miles an hour and you were going a lot faster than that!"

To this, my mom said in a voice that was getting more high pitched and louder with each syllable, *"Why Hell yeah, the speed limit is 40! But that don't mean backward you blue bellied son-of-a-b****!!!*

And with that, she stomped the gas and we were gone again, on our way to school, late as usual. For the rest of the ride to school that morning, my brother and I remained silent. We did not say a thing about the exchange we had just witnessed. But, when we got home that afternoon, we could not wait to tell our dad and sister about the incident. By then, we were all beginning to see the humor in the situation.

Of course, this incident had no impact on our school arrival times from that point on. My brother continued to be world-class at "assling around." My mom continued to drive like a bat out of hell on our daily commutes to school. And we continued to go around this same curve at way more than 40 miles per hour on a daily basis.

As luck and life would have it, a couple of things have kept this memory alive for me. First, as a school principal for 22 years, I had the opportunity to work with many students who were tardy on an everyday basis. I heard every excuse in the book for these tardy students, and I often thought of my brother, sister, and me during these discussions.

Also, this curve is within sight of my home today. Each morning as I head to work, I have to look down the road toward this same curve to check for traffic. Sometimes I see a vehicle coming around the curve at a rate of speed above the posted speed limit, which is still 40 miles per hour. Rarely do I pull out without thinking of my mom and the man on the truck that morning. It is one of those life memories that will always be with me. When I think of it, it always brings a smile to my face.

I have often thought about that man and what he was thinking after we left. He had just been spoken to very harshly by a mad, upset woman and was left standing in the middle of the road with no chance to even get in a word of self defense. I wonder if it was as funny to him at the end of the day as it was to us. Or if it is still funny to him, if he is alive, as it is to our family.

I have also wondered many times if a "blue-bellied son-of-a-b****" is worse than a "regular ol' son-of-a-b****"? I would say that the blue-bellied variety was at the top of the SOB list as far as my mom was concerned on this particular day.

Chapter 18

I SMELL CANE SYRUP COOKING

November is almost here and I can smell it in the air. It will soon be time to cook cane syrup.

For every year of my life that I can remember, there has been cane syrup cooked at the Lee family farm beginning around Thanksgiving. This happening each year on the farm is as predictable as any other seasonal sign that distinguishes one time of the year from another.

The beginning of the actual cooking of the syrup is preceded by many hours of labor and preparation. Like many other jobs on a farm, the process of changing pure cane juice from a green, sweet liquid freshly squeezed from the cane stalks into golden brown cane syrup, is hard work.

Dad, Silas and me doing the final cleaning of the pan before cooking cane syrup begins for the day.

Bill, Silas + Quincy
Nov. 25th 1977
day after Thanksgiving

The preparation process begins with the planting and tending of the cane. This part of the process is relatively easy since a cane patch, once planted, produces cane for several years in a row. As the time approaches to harvest the cane and get it ready to process, many other preparations have to take place.

The actual process of cooking down the cane juice into syrup requires heat – a lot of heat. After all, changing juice into syrup requires that approximately 90% of the water in the juice be evaporated in the cooking process. For many years now, my dad and his associates in the syrup making have used propane gas to provide the necessary heat to do the cooking. But, when I was a boy growing up on our farm, this wasn't the case.

While my brother, myself and a cousin of ours, who was a little older than us, was on the farm, there was a ready, though not necessarily willing, source of free labor. This labor was used by my dad and Uncle Homer to burst up large pieces of lightered wood that was burned under the syrup pan. These large lightered stumps had been harvested while clearing land many years earlier and piled into large woodpiles in various places around the farm. This wood was actually the stumps of old pine trees that had turned into "fat lightered." This wood is highly flammable and burns very hot, producing thick, black smoke as it burns. It also has a very distinctive odor, smelling like no other wood in the world. Once you have smelled "fat lightered" burning, you never forget that smell.

Hard as it may be to believe, we even used dynamite on the farm to help burst up some of these very large stumps into smaller pieces so that we were able to complete the process of cutting them into usable pieces with axes and awls. In fact, my dad had dynamite stored in one of the barns in a small, wooden box back in the 1960's. He would use a little at the time as was needed to help burst open some of the very largest stumps. He did this by drilling a hole in the stump, sticking a small amount of dynamite with a blast cap attached down into the hole and lighting a short length of fuse.

The unused dynamite stayed in that barn for many years after we quit using it, contained in that wooden box and sitting on a shelf in plain view of anyone who happened to pass by. We finally got rid of it in about 1985, being very careful to move it and properly dispose of it.

This process of bursting this lightered wood up was hard, tiring work. We would spend several days each year in September and October bursting the wood up and getting it moved closer to the cane mill. The bursting of the wood involved two people at the time with axes, one hitting one end of the stump and the other then hitting the other end of the stump, trying to make sure that the second ax was in the same groove or crack in the stump created by the first. We would also us an awl, an instrument that would be hammered into the crack in the stump, helping to hold it open and thereby making it easier to split. This process of splitting a stump up into usable pieces could take 30 minutes or more per stump.

As the cooking process would usually go on for several days and begin early each morning and last until late in the day, it was necessary to have a large supply of wood ready each year when the cooking began. Looking back on these days, it is sort of amazing to me how quickly my dad discovered the benefits of propane gas when my brother, my cousin and I grew up and were not available for the bursting of the wood. Of course my dad would probably say that they ran out of lightered was the only reason they started cooking with propane. Yeah, sure.

Anyway, once the heat supply has been prepared, it is time to get the cane ready. This is another task that has hard work all over it. First, the cane has to be stripped or have the leaves removed from the cane stalks. This requires that each and every stalk of cane in the entire field have the fodder removed, using a tool called a "stripper." This is a hand tool about 4 feet in length, with a metal tool instrument on the end shaped like a "V" with a slightly hooked end to it. Using this tool, a person would put the "V" shape around the top of the cane stalk, pulling it rapidly down the stalk, thereby removing all of the leaves of two sides of the stalk. Then this would be done again on the same stalk, changing to the side of the stalk that still had leaves attached. Once the leaves were removed from that single stalk of cane, the person doing the stripping would move to the next stalk. Because a single hill or cluster of cane can contain up to 10 or 12 stalks, one can see that this stripping of a field of cane can be very labor intensive.

When the stripping is completed, the next step is to "top" the cane. This process involves cutting the top of each stalk off at a place just above the last good joint, leaving only the part of the cane stalk that contains juice standing. Once this has been completed, the cane is then chopped down, using a hoe, machete or other sharp instrument and piled on the ground. It is then loaded onto a trailer and hauled to the mill area, where it is stacked on a platform, ready to be fed into the mill.

The cane grinding mill is a piece of machinery with large metal rollers through which the cane is passed, squeezing or pressing the juice from the stalk. This mill is powered by a tractor or other engine using a large belt and pulley system to turn the grinding gears. Feeding the cane mill is a really tiring job as it is constant. Once started each day, the cane mill has to be fed continuously until it is time to stop the cooking process for the day. Also, because it requires a large amount of juice each morning just to get started, the feeding of the mill often begins just after, sometimes even before, sun rise.

Cooking the syrup is actually a continuous process once it begins each day. Heat under the pan helps to evaporate the juice, changing it from the raw cane juice being emptied into the front of the cooking pan and changing it into cane syrup when it comes out of the spout at the other end. These cooking pans are usually about 12 feet in length and about 5 feet in width, having channels and baffles in each section of the pan to help channel the flow of the juice as it makes its way from one end of the pan to the other. The cooking of the syrup has to be monitored very carefully because it can quickly turn from syrup into sugar crystals if allowed to cook too long or if it is cooked at too high a temperature.

I can remember as a boy watching the steaming cane juice making its way through the pan, anxiously waiting for the first new syrup of the year. We would catch that first sample and take it straight to the house where my Ma and Pa, Momma, sister, brother and me would sit down to a breakfast of homemade biscuits, farm butter, hot cane syrup and some of my dad's homemade sausage. Dad would also join us, if he had enough help to keep the mill running while he ate breakfast. Then, one by one, the others who were working around the mill would make their way up to the house to sample the breakfast with the new syrup. I promise any breakfast that The Cracker Barrel or any other restaurant can fix comes up a far distant second to those breakfasts on the farm.

As the syrup was coming out of the pan, it would empty into a large wooden trough. It would then be allowed to cool down so that it could be handled. When cool enough, it would be poured into ½ gallon syrup cans, labeled and stacked. It would then be sold to area stores or to individuals who would come and buy the syrup.

This year, it may be difficult for syrup to be made at our farm because my dad had a stroke a few months back and I am not sure that there is anyone who can take up the slack to oversee the job. This may be one of those life moments when the inevitability of change makes itself known to our family one more time. But, if it happens that way, I will always have the recollections of making syrup with my family as one of my happy memories of life on the Lee Family Farm.

Chapter 19

DRUNK HOGS

G rowing up on a farm gives a person many opportunities to observe things that most people will never be able to see or experience. It would be impossible to compile a list of these learning opportunities as it would be very lengthy. But one that I did observe on more than one occasion was drunk hogs. Yep, that's right, stone cold drunk porkers!

Well, one may ask, how can it be that a bunch of hogs can get drunk? How can plain old pigs get a hold of the alcohol required to get drunk? Did a couple of them make a beer run in the late afternoon to the local convenience store? Maybe a couple got a fake I.D. from their friend at the next farm over and made the purchase at the local bar in town. Or perhaps, some of them knew a couple of good ol' pigs down the road who would furnish them with a little home-made hooch or moonshine that would do trick. No, none of these ways is how it came to be but the last one suggested may be pretty close.

For you see, while I was growing up on our family farm, one of the things we did every year that I can remember from the time I was a child until my dad was unable to do so anymore because of health issues was make home-made cane syrup. The making of this syrup produces a by-product known as the "skimmings" that are the impurities which are removed from the cane juice during the cooking process. These impurities are removed by workers using skimmers and dippers and placing the skimmed materials into large barrels located adjacent to the cooking pan.

Making cane syrup is usually a several day process with each day starting off with a fresh batch of cane juice that will be cooked down to the finished product of pure cane syrup. So, over the course of these several days, a large amount of impurities are skimmed during the cooking process. During a typical syrup making season, we would fill three or four 55 gallon drums with skimmings.

Most of the time, these skimmings would be used as a supplement for hog feed. We would mix shelled corn with the skimmings, let the mixture soak overnight so the corn would absorb the liquid and then feed it to the hogs the next day.

However, on more than one occasion, some of these skimmings would be loaded into the bed of a local person's pickup truck and he would drive away with a big smile on his face. On one of these occasions, I helped load the skimmings into the back of a pickup truck and the man drove away. Just a couple of weeks later, I was at my Uncle Homer's house visiting him and my Aunt Anne.

During the visit, he got up and went into another room and came back a minute or two later with a glass jar with a clear liquid in it. He opened it up and told me to take a sip or two. As I got the jar close to my nose, I could tell that it was real potent. It smelled just like cane juice and was as clear as pure water. But to say that it tasted anything like water would not be the truth. As they say, it burned all the way down!! Whew! White lightnin'! I asked Uncle Home where he got it and he named the fellow that I had helped load the skimmings.

Anyway, back to drunk hogs. When mixing these skimmings with the corn, we would only use a couple of gallons per day to mix with the corn. So, over a span of several days the skimmings, which had plenty of natural sugar in it, would begin to ferment before we would use it all up.

Therefore, when we would keep mixing the corn with the skimmings over a period of two or three weeks, the feed would become saturated with alcohol from the fermented skimmings. When the hogs would eat this mixture, they would get stone cold drunk. Sort of like moonshine for hogs.

Watching a bunch of drunk hogs can be real entertaining for a teenage boy. They act just like drunk people. Some are happy and others want to fight. Some want to wrestle and play and others want to sleep. A few will get up and try to walk, staggering around like the town alcoholic on Saturday night. Others will just lie around and grunt, looking like they are completely satisfied to just be left alone in their state of stupor.

I don't know if these drunk hogs developed hangovers or not. I do know the next day when it was feeding time, they all were eager for the next round of alcohol laced corn. They would eat the mixture with gusto and get drunk all over again.

I guess not many people can say they have had the pleasure of watching drunk hogs. Most people have never even thought of hogs being drunk. It is one of those funny and entertaining sights that are reserved only for those lucky enough to be raised on a farm.

Chapter 20

THE OLD WELL

The water supply for our family came from a dug well that sat just out the back door of our family home and about half-way between our back door and the front door to the small block home of my paternal grandparents, Silas and Della Lee or Pa and Ma. This well had been hand dug to a depth of about 35 or 40 feet many years before I was born by my Pa with the assistance of a cousin of his. This well was the only source of water for our family until my dad had a deep well installed at the farm several years after all of us children had left home.

According to the story my Pa told many times, the location for this well was determined using the "divinin' rod" method. This method is when a person walks around with a stick in the shape of a "Y" held firmly in the hands. When the "divining rod" turns down and points at the ground, with no conscience effort on the part of the holder, then that is the place to dig. I can't recall who the "diviner" was for this well but I do recall my Pa saying the person told him they would find water at 35 feet. I also remember Pa saying when they were digging the well with shovels, a pair of hole diggers and a pick axe, that as they got close to the 35 foot depth and would strike the hard dirt with the hole diggers or axe to loosen it for removal, it would sound like they were striking the head of a drum.

The man who was digging the well was down in the well shaft and the hollow sound became louder with each blow struck. He became concerned and had my Pa send a rope down to him and he tied it around his waist. He struck the dirt a few more times and then, with one blow, the hole diggers he was using burst through the bottom of the well and sunk up to almost the full length of the hole digger handles. He called out to my Pa to send a bucket down to get him out of there because the water started gushing into the well when he removed the hole diggers from the hole in the well floor.

According to Pa, before he could get a bucket down to the man to begin to pull him back up to the surface, the water was already chest deep on the man. Pa got the man out and within a few minutes, they measured the depth of the water in the well and found it to be about 15 feet deep. From that time on, the well never went dry nor had less than 12 to 15 feet of water in it at any time whether it was summer or winter, spring or fall, wet or dry, drought or no drought.

Early on, the family used a hand pump to get water out of the well but long before I was born, an electric pump had been installed to pump the water. The water from the well was naturally cool, clear and tasted great. The well was protected by a brick wall about 4 feet high built around it with wooden planks across the top of the enclosure to keep items or animals from falling into the well. The well was also covered with a small roof that kept out leaves and rain water.

However, once in a while, something would get into the well and have to be removed. Most of the time, these items would be some type of trash that had gathered on the boards and fell into the water through cracks between them. Once in a while, either a frog or maybe a field mouse would fall into the well and would have to be fished out with the well bucket and rope. But, one time something fell into the well that caused quite a problem and was the cause for one of the few times that I ever saw my dad get really sick.

We started noticing the problem when our water began to have a little bit of a cloudy look to it. Gradually, over a few days time, we also began to notice a slight odor to the water. Over these days, the water became cloudier and the odor became more pungent.

Thinking that maybe a frog had fallen into the well, my dad went out and removed the top boards from the well enclosure. Taking a flashlight in his hand, he shined it down the well shaft to see if he could tell what was in the water. He could not really tell what it was so he took the bucket and well rope and lowered it down with the winless to the water. He began to maneuver the bucket in an attempt to capture the item on top of the water and bring it up out of the well.

After some effort, he got the bucket around the item and started bringing the item up. When he got the bucket within about 8 to 10 feet of the top of the well, he could finally see what it contained. It was one of my Ma's old, dead, half-rotten pet cats. Oh, my gosh!! What a mess!!!

As my dad got the bucket with the dead cat in it closer and closer, he began to gag. Not just a small gag, but loud, long gags with each one getting more intense. He would pull the rope up a bit, gag, stop, pull on the rope, gag some more and so on until the bucket and cat was at the top of the well. At this point, my dad reached out and grabbed the bucket and gave it a sling.

About this time, I believe the realization of what we had been drinking for the last few days hit my dad. He would take a couple of steps, heave with all his might, say a few choice words, wipe his mouth, take a few more steps, curse some more, gag some more, curse a little more, throw up some and try to catch his breath to start all over again. Gagging, walking, cursing, gagging, lots of choice words, throwing up. This little routine went on for a few minutes until finally dad was able to stop the gagging and throwing up.

I don't remember how the dead, stinking, rotten cat was finally re-moved from the well bucket and disposed of or by whom. I do remember that my dad poured a couple of jugs of pure Clorox bleach down the well and turned on every faucet on the farm and let them run for the next couple of days to rid the well of all the rotten water we had been drinking. My mom went to town and bought us several gallon jugs of distilled water to drink. This was the first time that I can remember drinking bought water. He also had a man by the name of Rupert Padgett, who worked at the local health department with my mother, to come out and test the water several times over the next few days.

After this episode, dad did a little extra work around the well enclo-sure to make sure that a similar incident did not happen again. As a mat-ter of fact, after the repair job completed, I am not sure that a flea could have gotten into the well. Anyway, after a few days time, we began to see the humor in the situation, especially when we began to recall the show that my dad had put on for us when removing the cat. Seeing a man as tough as my man who prided himself in being able to handle almost any-thing reduced to gagging, heaving, cursing, spitting, throwing up, gag-ging some more, cursing some more and so on was a really funny sight. We also tried to make sure that we did a little better job of keeping up with Ma's cats from then on.

Chapter 21

OL' DAISY LOVED THEM TOMATOES

I must say at the age of 55 when writing this, I have a totally different outlook on the events I am about to tell about than I had on the day it happened at around the age of 12 or so. I am also thankful for forgiveness for some acts committed during my years of youth on the farm that fell somewhere short of proper behavior. So, here goes the story of a prank pulled as a young fella that was dang funny to a bunch of ol' farm boys then that may not be quite so funny now.

Most of the folks that lived around our neck of the woods had a mule or horse which they used to help do the gardening. This was especially true of those people who did not have the means to buy a tractor. Though we did have several tractors on our farm, dad also kept ol' Daisy around so, as dad would say to anyone listening, "Just in case times ever get hard again, like they were during the great depression when I was growing up and during World War II, when gas was not available". (We had all heard this speech so many times we could almost quote it word for word, including the facial expressions.)

He put this belief into action also as he made sure that my brother Silas, my first cousin Sammy, and me all learned to plow with Daisy, in-cluding how to put on all of the required components such as the bridle, bit, mule collar, plow lines, etc. He taught us the proper handling of the plows and how to speak to the ol' mule as she was going along, with "gee" meaning for the mule to turn to the right, "haw" for the mule to turn to the left, "geddup" for go, and "Whoa!" for stop.

Though I did not have to do a lot of plowing with the old mule, I did it enough to develop a real appreciation for the fact that men had actually done this for days at the time in the not too distant past in order to plant their entire farms to eke out a living for their families. It is no wonder that those folks did not have much fat on their bodies doing that kind of work.

Anyway, ol' Daisy was our mule and had been on our farm for many years, way before I was born. One of my jobs as a boy was to feed and water Daisy and our horse, Bob, every day in the afternoon after school or during the summer.

They both loved corn, corn shucks, and hay. During the spring and summer, when the gardens were producing, they also enjoyed eating fresh vegetables that we would throw out to them. In particular, ol' Daisy loved tomatoes. She would eat them just about as long as you would provide them.

Now the place that Daisy and Bob stayed in consisted of a small stall area with a couple of covered pens where they stayed during the night and a corral area that was surrounded by a single wire of electric fence. They would not come close to the fence most of the time because it would really "bite" if it was touched.

One day, as I was preparing to give some tomatoes to Daisy, an idea struck me. Looking back, I am sure this was an example of when too much time, too little to do, several boys looking for cheap entertainment, and a "willing" participant combined for a prank on an unsuspecting victim.

Knowing how much Daisy loved tomatoes, I decided that I would see just how badly she wanted to eat one. I took out my pocket knife, which I always had with me, and sliced a single tomato just one time like I was going to cut it in half, except that I only went about half-way. I then had one of my friends turn off the electric fence momentarily and slipped the tomato onto the fence where it was just sitting there. The fence was turned back on.

I then tossed some other tomatoes into the area in the pen by the tomato on the fence and called ol' Daisy. In just a minute, here she came. She quickly started eating the tomatoes on the ground and finished them up in a matter of a few minutes. Then the fun started.

She smelled the tomato on the fence and started to reach over and take a bite. Just as she did, the electric fence delivered its juice. The poor old mule's lips just started to quiver as she tried to eat the tomato. She backed off for a couple of seconds and then gave it another go. Again, her lips just quivered as she tried to eat her favorite snack but she could not get her mouth to the tomato without feeling the jolt of electricity. She backed off again.

By this time, those of us watching this sight were really enjoying the prank at the expense of the mule. I know one of the reasons we were enjoying it was that most of us had also been tricked at one time or another to get into an electric fence by some of our friends. After watching a few more attempts by Daisy to eat the tomato, I knocked it off the fence and let her have it.

To be honest with you, it was dang funny at the time, maybe not so much now. It is a truism of life that idle time, mischievous kids, clever minds, and the opportunity to combine all of these sometimes leads to less than proper behavior. Thankfully, most of us survive these times with no lasting effects or scars. Perhaps it is more important that we learn to look back on these time and try to teach our own children to "do unto others as you would have them to do unto you" and maybe remember when this lesson was learned by us.

Chapter 22

CORN COBS AND IRISH POTATOES –
DODGE BALL COUNTRY STYLE

Y ou learn some things while being raised in the country on a family farm that city kids just don't get to learn. There are way too many of these to try to make an exhaustive list but one that comes to my mind right now is how to have a lot of fun playing a country game of "dodge ball" when the "balls" that are being used are wet pieces of corn cob and small Irish potatoes, fresh from the garden.

It is said that necessity is the mother of invention. And since there were no real balls available when this type of country dodge ball was invented, sometime many years ago some brilliant child came up with the idea of substituting pieces of corn cob soaked in water or small Irish potatoes for a real ball.

Most everyone knows how the game of dodge ball is played. Players either choose up sides and compete against one another as teams or some participants are selected as the throwers and everyone else gets in the "ring" and tries to dodge the balls as they are thrown.

In the country game of dodge ball, we always picked teams and competed against one another in that way. Several kids would be on each team and the "balls" to be used depended upon the time of year. In the spring, just after the potatoes had been gathered into the barn and spread out so as not to rot, the "ball" of choice was small, round, red Irish potatoes. These were excellent as they were of fairly uniform shape and size and could really be thrown at each other quite accurately. And, when you were hit by one of these, you blame well knew it! It would hurt like the dickens.

But, just as in regular games of dodge ball, no whining was allowed in our games of country dodge ball. *You were allowed* to rub the spot for just a minute or two if absolutely necessary.

Using the potatoes as substitutes for balls had one little drawback. That was my Ma, who was my paternal grandmother, would just about skin you for using those new potatoes for balls after she had helped do the work to gather them up and have them ready for food. It was best for us to do this only when we were absolutely sure that Ma was not around.

In the fall of the year, the ball of choice for these games of dodge ball was often pieces of corn cob left over from shelling the corn for chicken feed. These pieces of corn cob would be broken up into lengths about 2 to 3 inches long and then soaked in water to give them a little extra weight. There was a good thing and bad thing about using these corn cobs as substitutes for the balls. The good thing was because of their irregular shape, they were not as accurate as the potatoes, and therefore you did not get hit as often. The bad thing though was that if you ever did get hit with one of these corn cob pieces, it would hurt! A corn cob thrown by an older kid at about the same velocity as a baseball will dang well draw up a knot on you where ever it makes contact! And, this mark on your body would serve as proof that you were out of the game. Many a game of corn cob dodge ball ended after the first round because all of the participants were less than anxious to get hit by these flying inflictors of pain again.

After reading this, if any of you feel deprived because you did not get to experience a country game of dodge ball since you were raised in the city, it will be real easy to correct this deficiency in your raising. Just go to your local grocery store, get you some small Irish potatoes and a few ears of corn on the cob. Eat the corn and save the cobs. Break them into short pieces about 2 to 3 inches long and soak them in water.

Give me a call. I will gather up a few folks who will be happy to be the designated throwers and will meet you at a place of your choosing for the game. This country game of dodge ball will allow you to fully participate in this life learning experience.

Remember, no whining allowed. Just get in the ring or choose up sides.

Chapter 23

SOMETIME BETWEEN PLANTING POTATOES AND COOKING CRACKLINGS

S ometime between the planting of potatoes in the early spring and the cooking of the cracklings in the dead of winter, the cycle of life on the Lee family farm took place. These events marked the beginning of the renewal of life each year and the end of the harvest season when all of the work on the farm for the year came to conclusion. Much of the essence of life revolved around these seasons of the year from the time my grandparents, Silas and Della Lee, homesteaded the property in about 1912 until well after their passing in 1966. This anticipation of the events of the seasons were as regular as one of my Ma's old roosters crowing at the sun coming up each morning and the cows coming to the barn in the late afternoon. Many of these seasonal events were guided by the times, dates, moon phases and suggestions in the Old Farmer's Almanac.

Potatoes were the first crops in the ground each year, always being planted on or very close to Valentine's Day. My Ma made sure the seed potatoes were ready for planting each spring and when it was time, the potatoes would go into the ground, eyes up as long as she was alive. She would speak harshly to you if she caught you dropping potatoes into the furrow with the eyes (sprouts) of the cuttings down. Her belief was those eyes needed to be facing toward the sun for the potato crop to produce to its fullest capacity though in fact, the potatoes will come up just as well either way.

English peas (sweet peas) would be planted shortly after the potatoes with the other spring crops following close behind such as corn, okra, and butter beans. Peas of various varieties, such as Cream 40, Purple Hull, Black-eyed, little White Acre and Zipper peas would also be planted. The reason for the variety of peas is that each type has unique qualities in terms of taste, size, shelling and growing seasons. For example, young Sweet Peas can be picked and cooked without being shelled. Add some freshly dug new potatoes and maybe some fried chicken, late winter turnips or mustard greens, some corn bread, banana pudding and a pitcher of sweet tea and you have a meal fit for a king.

On the other hand, little white acre peas are very small peas at maturity, harder to pick, harder to shell, produce less quantity but are really delicious when mixed with some fresh cream corn. Purple hull peas, on the other hand, are much larger, produce more on the vine, are much easier to shell, but are not quite as good, at least to me, as the little white peas. But, if I am going to have to shell them before I get to eat them, then, bring on the purple hulls and let me have to suffer with a little less taste.

Of all of the variety of peas and beans that we grew, the ones that I loved to eat but hated like heck to have to pick or shell, it would be butterbeans. Butterbean bushes grow close to the ground and the beans on the plants are located close to the vine making them hard to reach to pick. On top of that, the actual butter bean is a small pod, usually containing 3 or 4 individual beans with the hulls shaped sort of like a half moon and very flat. You can pick butter beans for a long time in the garden and not even come close to having a bucket full. And, even after they are picked, the fun has just begun. Shelling butter beans is aggravating as they are hard to open, they have a pointed, sharp end that will gouge your fingers and it takes about 5 gallons of picked beans to make up a "mess of beans" for eating. But, when cooked just right, I must say they are dang sure good.

Of course, seed going into the ground to begin growing is just one sign of the renewal of life on a farm. About the same time as the planting started, the farm animals started giving birth to the baby animals or the eggs under an old setting hen would hatch. I can remember many times when my Ma would have cardboard boxes of little, yellow chicks sitting in her kitchen by the stove with a light on them to help keep them warm, watching them grow and get big enough to be placed into the little chicken coop, complete with water bottles and feed troughs located under the barn. The brood cows would all have new calves within a few days of one another, the hogs would have new litters of pigs and you could see thousands of tadpoles swimming along the edges in the farm pond.

Other plants would also be in full bloom such as peach trees, pear trees, fig trees, blueberry bushes and wild briars from which large amounts of blackberries could be picked. All of these fruits would be picked, washed, processed and cooked into jellies, jams, and preserves by my grandparents, mom, dad, aunts and uncles with the help of a little free, though not always willing, labor from all of the children. There is nothing that can be bought in any store that even comes close to the taste of these home-made jellies, jams, and preserves when spread on a hot, buttermilk biscuit or on a piece of toast in the morning with breakfast.

One of the tasty treats that I remember that used some of this home-made jelly was a cake my Aunt Anne would cook. She would cook several small, thin layers of a yellow cake batter. Then she would stir up some jelly until it was very smooth, almost like syrup. She would then spread the jelly/syrup between the layers of the cake like an icing, allowing it to seep down into the cake layers. She would serve it, while it was still warm if you were there at the right time, in slices accompanied by a big glass of cold milk. My goodness was that ever delicious!!

As spring turns to summer, the changing times bring along with it changes on the farm. The corn starts to mature and change from food for us to eat to the crop that will be harvested to feed the animals during the fall and winter. The little chicks grow into small hens and begin laying eggs. The heifer (female) calves mature and soon have calves of their own and the bull claves are either sold or made into steers to be fattened up for slaughter and turned into steaks and hamburger. The piglets become feeder pigs and gain weight at a rapid rate, being fed on corn and hog pellets and not having a clue that winter is coming when they will be required to make the supreme sacrifice for the Lee family.

The old comparison of the difference in the commitment of a chicken and pig to a family breakfast on the farm has a whole lot of truth to it to demonstrate the difference in a partial or total commitment. In life, like the chicken that lays an egg, sometimes we are able to make a partial commitment and it is perfectly fine. But, at other times, like the poor old hog supplying the ham, life asks us to make a total commitment to obtain the desired goal or to reach our destination. I suppose that partial commitments are okay for many of life's demands but it is when we have to make total commitments that probably help us to keep moving on when life presents the challenges that come to all humans.

Summer turns to fall and life moves on. Fruits and vegetables have been picked and put up, either canned or frozen, and stored for use in the months ahead. The corn has been picked and is in the barn, being used on a daily basis for feeding the chickens, hogs, cows, horse and Ol' Daisy, the farm mule. The hay has been cut and put in the loft to feed the cows through the winter. The sugar cane is ready for harvest and will shortly be cooked down to some sweet, delicious homemade syrup. A few late fall crops, like turnips, mustard and collards are planted and will be ready in a few weeks, just before the first frost of winter. And the hogs are still getting their fix of corn and hog pellets, gaining weight every day. Winter is coming.

The older folks would check the Old Farmer's Almanac, listen to the radio and watch the local weather news on TV, to see when it was going to turn really cold, looking for the right time to do a hog killing. The time draweth nigh for the piglets, turned feeder pigs, turned fully grown hogs to do their part in support of the Lee family food chain. This winter-time event, in which sometimes as many as 8 or more swine would be processed into meat by several different family members, usually happened on a weekend taking both Saturday and Sunday. It was always a lot of work and produced all of the regular types of pork meat one would expect such as ham, bacon, pork roast, pork chops and pork loin. Of course, out in the country, we saved everything but the oink. So, in addition to the items listed above, we also would have hog-head cheese, hash, pig ears, liver, pickled pig feet, and those tasty treats that only southern folks could love, chittlins' (chitterlings).

Usually, the last item to be processed from one of these hog killing times was the cooking of the cracklings. Cracklings are actually produced by trimming most of the fat away from the skin of the pork, cutting the skin into small squares, 1 to 2 inches wide, and placing these small pieces into a pot and cooking them. On the Lee farm, this cooking was done in an old, cast iron pot that held about 15 gallons which looked exactly like a "witches brew" pot from Halloween or in the large cast iron syrup kettle that would hold 150 gallons or more. Once the small pieces of meat had been added to the pot, a fire would be started and the cracklings would be cooked until golden brown. They would then be removed from the pot, leaving behind a large quantity of grease or "hog lard." This grease would be allowed to cool, placed into jars and used in the months ahead just like any other type of cooking oil like Crisco, peanut oil, or corn oil. The cracklings would be either be eaten, like modern day pork rinds, mixed in and cooked with corn-bread (crackling bread) or frozen for future use.

The cracklings have been cooked. The sun begins to come up a minute or two earlier each day and it goes down a minute or two later. The bitter cold days don't come as often. Robins can be seen flying in a northerly direction. Walking through the pasture when gathering the cows to the barn, there are a few, very small, purple violets visible in the brown grass. The month of January is almost over and February will be here in just a few days. After that, Valentine's Day. Time to plant potatoes.

And so, the cycle starts again. Before long, the potatoes will be planted and spring will be in full bloom. Shortly thereafter, the heat of summer will be like a furnace. The colors of fall will come pretty quickly. The leaves will fall from the trees and the frost of a cold, winter morning will be on the ground.

It will soon be time to cook the cracklings

Chapter 24

HONEY, HAVE YOU EVER....

My Aunt Annie Rosa Lee was one of the most influential people in my life when I was growing up. She was the lady who kept us children every day after school until my mom would get home from her job as a nurse with the Holmes County Health Department. In fact, my Aunt Anne actually would come to our home every morning shortly after we would leave for school and serve as the "lady of the farm" by doing all of the things necessary each day to help keep the family farm going. These included helping with the gardening, washing clothes, canning fruits and vegetables during season, cooking dinner meals every day for my Uncle Homer, Ma and Pa (my paternal grandparents) and others who may have been helping around the farm on any particular day, cleaning the house for our family, sweeping the yards, mending clothes or whatever else needed to be done. She was also there every day when all of us children would get off of the school bus, waiting with a big hug, a snack on the table and love in her heart.

Among the many things she did, perhaps the most important was she helped to teach all of us a moral set of values and beliefs that were founded on the Biblical principles of love, fairness, treating people right, honesty, faith, and the importance of family and friends. She taught us these by living them before us each day and by telling us often when one of the teaching moments of life presented itself. She was never rich in any sense of the word in material possessions. She was rich beyond measure in faith and goodness and in helping others.

One of the things that she often did when she would be conversing with someone was start the conversation with the word honey. As in "Honey, did you remember to do your homework?" or "Honey, would you please help me by taking the clothes out there to the wash shed?" I guess this was just one of her words of kindness that I remember as she lived her life day to day.

So, in honor to my Aunt Anne and having been considering a few things about life over the last few days, here are a few questions that may bring back a memory or two to some of you who may have been lucky enough to have been born and raised in the country.

Honey, have you ever ....
Taken clothes off of the clothesline after they have been hanging out drying for a few hours and smelled the freshness of the clean, country air in the clothes?

Honey, have you ever....
Walked through the garden and picked a "tommy toe" tomato (cherry tomato) off a vine, rubbed any dirt or grime off of it on your clothing, popped the whole thing in your mouth as you walked along, biting down and letting the juices explode on your taste buds, perhaps even having a trickle run down from the corners of your mouth onto your chin and wiping the juice with the sleeve of your shirt as you continued on your way?

Honey, have you ever....
Dove into a cold, spring fed creek with nothing on but a pair of cut off blue jeans in the middle of July and had the cold, cold water take your

breath away momentarily from the sudden change from 95 degrees to 68 degrees on your body?

Honey, have you ever…

Been swimming in that cold, cold water and eagerly waiting to cut the big watermelon that was brought from home which is laying just in the edge of the water chilling among some tree roots. When it is cut up into slices, you slurp a big piece as the juice runs down your chin, your hands and arms with no worry as all will be washed off when you dive under the water again.

Honey, have you ever…..

Walked through the barnyard, barefooted as the day you were born, and stepped into a fresh little pile of chicken manure that was squeezed up between your toes, hollered at the top of your lungs and did a quick rendition of a dance known as the barn yard shuffle in the nearest patch of grass or used the closest water spigot to remove said chicken manure from your toes.

Honey, have you ever…..

Sat on the porch of an old farm house and listened to the old folks talk about friends and relations from the past and wondered how they could remember all of those people and things that happened so long ago and been amazed at how these tales of times past would seem to cause some of them to linger in their thoughts, perhaps even shed a small tear, as they would reminisce.

Honey, have you ever…..

Sat on that same porch with those same people watching and listening to a sudden southern thunder storm roll across the countryside complete with lightening popping, thunder rolling and rain drops the size of quarters splashing all around and being amazed at how quickly it came and how quickly it went.

Honey, have you ever.....

Grabbed hold of a cow's tail and held on for dear life as she would take off running across a pasture and attempt to "grass ski" for as long as you could before losing your balance and falling down or having the cow to make a sudden turn and leave you tumbling across the pasture. By the way, sometimes these "grass skiing" adventures would take you and your feet directly through freshly deposited piles of cow manure. For the response to this, go back a few paragraphs and read about chickens in a barnyard.

Honey, have you ever....

Picked little purple violets out of a pasture in the early spring and been amazed that these small flowers would be peeking out of the ground at times when there would still be frost on the ground from time to time.

Honey, have you ever.....

Started playing a game of hide and go seek or chase with a herd of cousins and friends on an early summer evening and having the game change right in the middle to a game of catching fire flies and putting them in a quart jar as the light would fade and the lightening bugs would be flashing all around.

Honey, have you ever....

Picked cotton and let the smell of the fresh cotton fill your nostrils as it is piled up on the back porch of an old farm house or loaded into the back of a rattle-trap pickup truck just before heading off to the cotton gin to be sold and processed.

Honey, have you ever……

Participated in an old fashioned, sitting up with the dead, wake when funeral homes would bring the recently departed loved one home to lie in state for a period of time, often in their own beds, while family, loved ones and friends would stop by and offer condolences to the immediate family, sometimes over a period of a few days. During this wake, it would often fall to some family member and perhaps a close friend, to sit up with the dead overnight each night that the recently departed one remained at the home. (I guess they were assigned to keep an eye on him or her, just in case they decided to go on a journey or came back to life.)

Honey, have you ever…..

Been chased around a barnyard by a mad setting hen shortly after she has finished hatching a setting of eggs because she thinks you are a threat to her new born chicks.

Honey, have you ever…..

Been fishing with just you and your grandma at a small farm pond when she was teaching you how to bait a hook and take fish off the hook, all the while telling you about the best ways and times to fish including a few words of wisdom such as these –

Winds from the east, fish bite the least.
Winds from the west, fish bite the best.
Winds from the south, blows the bait in their mouth.

Since there were no words about winds from the north, I would guess that means fishing when the wind was from the north would just be a waste of time.

Honey, have you ever....

Helped wash clothes outside in the washroom on an old fashioned wringer type washing machine which required the clothes to be washed, rinsed and then run through a squeezing mechanism to remove all of the excess water before the clothes could be hung out to dry on one of several clothes lines that were nearby. Once, while doing this, I got my hand caught in the wringer (squeezer) and it was rolling my hand and arm up through the wringer until my Aunt Anne quickly reversed the rollers and rolled my hand and arm right back out. You don't have to do this but a couple of times before you learn not to get your hands and fingers caught in these rollers.

Honey, have you ever....

Witnessed a person being baptized (or maybe even been the one being baptized) in the cold water of a local creek while a group of church members, family and friends are gathered on the shore singing old time gospel favorites as the newest member of the church is baptized into the fellowship of believers.

Honey, have you ever....

Been woke up by the sound of a single rooster crowing loudly at the crack of dawn as the sun turns the early morning sky bright red as it chases the darkness away, wishing that the dang rooster would just shut up and getting instead, a chorus of roosters joining the first rooster in welcoming the new day.

Honey, have you ever......

Stood by the fireplace on a cold winter night, warming yourself and your pajamas on both sides before running down the hall and jumping into the coolness of the bed while pulling the sheets, several blankets and the bedspread up tightly around you to help you stay warm in a bedroom that had no heat of any kind?

Honey, have you ever.....

Jumped out of bed on a cold winter morning and ran down the hall to the fireplace to warm up and being thankful that your dad was there to start the fire that morning and had it burning brightly when you got up and at the same time smelling homemade sausage cooking on the stove, seeing cat head biscuits sitting on the table and answering the only question that mattered at the time – "Do you want your eggs fried or scrambled?"

Honey, have you ever......

Watched a calf being born, watched as kittens open their eyes for the first time, seen a hawk dive down to catch a field mice or small rabbit, listened to bob white quails whistle in the early morning hours, heard the whippoorwill's song on a clear, cool night, been to a "Sacred Harp" sing, attended a tent or brush arbor revival, heard a coon dog's howl as he strikes a fresh trail, helped with cooking cane syrup, shucked corn with your grandpa to feed the horse and mule, seen thousands of tad-poles swimming at the edge of a farm pond, dammed up a small creek just for the fun of it, went skinny dipping in a creek on a dare, smelled "cracklings" cooking in a cast iron wash pot, heard the crowing of a young rooster at dawn, stood in a pasture and watched thousands of black birds flying south for the winter or north for the summer.

Well, honey, have you?
I have.

Chapter 25

GERTRUDE AND QUINCY
NEVER READ DR. SPOCK

D r. Benjamin Spock wrote several books on parenting skills and raising children. One of these books, first published in 1946 entitled
"Baby and Child Care" presented new and radically different thoughts on
how parents should rear children. Some of these suggestions included
such ideas as allowing children to be more independent in response to
parental directions, permitting children to express themselves when they
did not agree with parental decisions and advocating disciplinary measures that did not include spanking a child for misbehavior.

Gertrude and Quincy never read this book.

Nor did they read any of the other books that Dr. Spock may have published
about how to raise children. I am not sure they ever read any book about
raising children not counting the Bible. Based on their actions from time to
time, I do believe they were pretty familiar with the 10 Commandments,
especially the ones beginning with the "Thou Shalt Nots." I also am pretty

sure they had read a few select verses from Proverbs about sparing the rod and spoiling the child and children are to obey their parents.

My brother Silas, my sister Janis and I have discussed the parenting skills of our parents many times in the years since we have been adults and had children of our own. These discussions almost always revolve around some incident in which one of us was the recipient of "parenting" on the part of our parents and are followed most of the time by laughter, additional memories and a true sense of thankfulness for the blessing we had by having a good momma and daddy.

But the parenting skills used by momma and daddy were not those in the books of Dr. Spock or any other psychologist. In fact, many of the parenting practices used by my parents were those of the tried, true, and traditional ways of raising children. A few of these are explained in the following paragraphs.

When my parents spoke and told you something to do, it wasn't in the form of a suggestion. Both of my parents had total understanding of the English language when speaking to their children and this understanding was if they told us something to do, it was to be done. End of discussion. No if, ands or buts need apply. Just get up and get moving.

Mom and dad also had never heard of the "count to 3 rule" when they told us children to do something. If they had, then they always skipped numbers 1 and 2, moving right quick to number 3! You might get a gentle, or maybe not so gentle, reminder on occasion, but that was more the exception than the rule. Most of the time they worked pretty hard on that part of our character called obedience. That is doing what you are told to do when you are told to do it. As in right now.

Like most children, we would sometimes procrastinate, put off or just forget to do something like take out the trash or feed the dogs. When these types of situations would arise, mom would be gentle in her reminders most of the time. She might say something like, "Bill, did you remember to feed the dogs this afternoon?" as a reminder to do one of my daily chores. But, she also had a well developed ability to get your attention and put you into action when needed by raising her voice a few decibels or speaking in, shall we say, plain English.

My dad could also be patient on occasion when one of us would not mind in a timely manner. On other occasions, he might increase the volume on his voice a little or speak with a little more firmness in his voice as a reminder to complete a chore or follow directions. But, when necessary, he also had the ability to very clearly articulate instructions to us in ways that were, shall we say, easily understood with complete clarity. At times like these, we dang sure didn't need an interpreter to understand what dad was saying. After all, how hard is it to understand something like, "Get your ass out of this house right now and feed them dogs!" Even folks lacking basic language skills can understand instructions like that.

Another thing my parents stressed in our growing up years was to respect our elders, parents, grandparents, aunts, uncles and other kin folks. My mom and dad expected us to address all adults with whom we would come into contact with a "sir" or "ma'am" in any conversation with them especially in terms of answering questions from them. If an adult asked one of us children a question, any answer that did not come with a "Yes, sir", "No, sir.", "Yes, ma'am." or "No, ma'am." was met with a swift and sure correction from either mom or dad. If mom or dad was the adult talking to us, it was not good for our immediate health if our answers were less than acceptable. This habit has been so well ingrained into all of us that we still, even as adults, tend to address those people older than us in this same manner.

The respect for elders was also stressed in other ways. Both mom and dad taught us from birth that our grandparents and other adult kin folks were to be honored because of their status as family members. Talking back to or disrespecting one of these family members was taken as a serious offense and was cause for sure and swift discipline. As a matter of fact, the last whipping (spanking) that I ever received from my dad was for talking back to my grandmother, his mom. This is how this came to be.

Dad and mom were away from home for the day and my dear, sweet, sister Janis, who is only 5 years older than me, was supposed to be watching me. Sometime during the day, she told me to do something that I did not want to do. I don't remember what it was but just imagine a brother and sister arguing about one telling the other one something to do!!

Anyway, she went and told my Ma that I wouldn't mind her. So, Ma came over and told me to do it and I responded with something like "Aw, Ma, I don't want to do that." Really, this was all I said but I guess that was all it took.

Anyway, when my dad got home, my dear, sweet, sister Janis told him that I had talked back to Ma. This information was met with the expected response, that being that Dad and I had a real close personal encounter immediately after getting the report. Right after that, I had a completely clear understanding of how serious he took this talking back to my grandmother. In fact, I marked it right off my "bucket list" of things to do in life. I had done that one and didn't plan on doing it again!!

Our parents also taught us that work was an honorable thing and helped us to understand this concept by having us actually work while we were growing up. Imagine that, a set of cruel, heartless, mean parents who made their children work and do chores while they were growing up!! Silas and I had several chores including feeding and caring for the livestock on the farm and milking the cows every morning. We also had to help on the farm by plowing fields, picking vegetables, helping with the harvesting of the crops and performing numerous other farm related chores.

One of the jobs that I dreaded each year at the beginning of summer was the annual cleaning of the fence rows that ran around the perimeter of our property along the dirt roads. This involved starting at the home place and using hoes, axes, saws and whatever else was required to completely remove all vegetation from the fences that surrounded our property along the roads adjacent to our home. This chore would take 2 to 3 weeks to complete each summer and was hot, exhausting work. What is amazing to Silas and me now is that as soon as we left home, this chore was left undone for a few years and then my dad discovered herbicide!! Will wonders never cease?

Janis also had chores to do being required to do many of the household chores such as ironing, cleaning house and washing clothes. She was doing these chores when there were no permanent press clothes, we didn't own a vacuum cleaner and the clothes dryer we had was the sunshine. What is really funny about this is that both mom and dad thought this was good for our development and would help us to understand that life was filled with responsibilities. How old fashioned!!

I could go on for many more paragraphs about the parenting skills of Gertrude and Quincy Lee. They could give children instructions in easy to understand language. They actually expected children to be obedient. They believed in and taught respect for elders. They believed that work never hurt anyone. They expected us to fulfill the responsibilities that had been given to us. They actually punished us for not obeying, for being disrespectful and for not fulfilling our obligations. And they dang sure didn't spend any time psychoanalyzing how these expectations affected our inner-self or worrying about if our feelings might have been hurt or not.

While serving as a high school principal for 22 years, I had the opportunity to observe and interact with many parents and children. I must say that many of these observations and interactions came about because of family issues involving children that were having behavioral problems either at school, at home, or both. During these conversations, I saw many children disrespect their parents in more ways than I care to relate here. I watched many times as parents would take up for or make excuses for children who were in severe need of discipline. I even heard many parents say things like, 'I can't do a thing with him (or her)." Without fail, when I was involved in these types of meetings, I wanted to say to many parents and students, "What that child should have had was the opportunity to be raised at Route 1, Bonifay, Florida by Quincy and Gertrude Lee and he (she) would be acting a whole lot different than they are now."

In closing, I want to say, I have had many, many blessings in this life. The good Lord has blessed me in ways beyond measure and I have not the words to adequately express how grateful I am for these blessings. But, without a doubt the best blessing that He ever gave me was the one of having Gertrude and Quincy Lee as parents.

Though they never read any of the books by Dr. Spock, they were great parents in every way. My prayer and hope would be that one day, at the time in their lives when they have the chance to reflect on life, my own children can say the same thing about me and my wife.

That is they had a great dad and mom who, by the way, never read Dr. Spock either.

Chapter 26

MOMMA GASES DAD

My parents had a unique relationship. I suppose this can be said for all married couples that live together for over 50 years as did my mom and dad. I liken these relationships to a finely practiced dance routine with each partner knowing the other's moves, moods, steps and stops.

One of the givens of the choreography between my mom and dad was that my dad was the one more apt to pull a practical joke on my mom. But, on a few occasions, my mom paid him back dearly.

One night as they were lying in bed, getting ready for sleep, my mom acted as if she had a huge cough complete with the production of a large amount of saliva. She then began to tell my dad that she was just going to spit straight up into the air and let it land where it would. My dad kept telling her she better not do it but the threats continued.

Unbeknownst to by dad, mother had been faking the cough and saliva in her mouth as a plan. Also, unbeknownst to him, she had been having a little, make that a big, gas problem before he came to bed. And, lastly, unbeknownst to him, she had released a large portion of this gas under the cover just before faking the cough in one of the great SBD (Silent But Deadly) gas attacks of all time.

Well, as she was acting just like she was going to go through with the spitting straight up into the air, my dad dived under the cover. The rest, as they say is history.

Upon going under cover, he discovered that he had been gassed. This gas was almost as bad as tear gas. It certainly clouded up his eyes, filled his lungs and burned his nostrils.

The covers flew back, a few choice words were used and the lady, who seldom got the best of the practical jokes around our house, had the laugh of her life. My dad took it like a man and enjoyed the laugh, also. He was always one who could take as well as give.

She could not wait to share this with everyone she saw for the next few days. Of course, one of my dad's favorite sayings was, "Let your conscience be your guide because you know that I am going to pay you back." So, she probably knew that he would be good to his word on this philosophy.

I am sure that at some time, he did something to my mom that he considered payback for being gassed. But, you know how it is trying to pay someone back for a practical joke. The payback just never quite measures up to the original.

Chapter 27

CORB MARTIN TEACHES DAD A LESSON

My dad was one of those people in life who loved a good practical joke, whether it was on him or someone else. He just looked for ways to pull one over on people that were around him for any length of time and he would do just about anything to pull a prank on someone.

One of his favorite practical jokes was to spray water on some unsuspecting soul who would be around him working. Sometimes, the spray game would just be a light misting. Other times, he would wet you down or at least until you were out of reach of the water hose. He really loved to do this if it was cold weather when it happened so that the victim of the prank would have to wear wet clothes on a chilly day. It did not bother him in the least if the favor was returned. He would just laugh and go on about his work. And, if someone made a fuss about getting sprayed, well, to dad, this was just a sign to see if he could do it again, maybe even better.

He would do this "water spray" trick to just about anyone. Some of the ones that he really loved to do this to were the grand kids, especially my nephews Chris and Brad, when they were little. They would take off running and do their best to pay him back, which he enjoyed even more.

Everyone who worked around dad knew of this habit of his. Every once in a while, some of these people would "get the drop" on dad and spray him first. Most of the time, when this happened, he would just sit there and take it. But, this always came with a warning. He would always, and I mean always, say with a smile on his face, "You know that is going to cost you. I will pay you back!" As with most other things in his life, he was a man of his word. He would pay you back.

One day, several of us were at the farm helping to butcher a steer. We had just got started with the process of skinning the steer, when dad started up with the spraying water tricks. He got a couple of us pretty good, smiling all the time.

One of the people that was helping with this process was a man by the name of Corb Martin. Now Corb had worked many times at the farm with dad in various endeavors and he knew my dad well. The first time dad sprayed Corb that day, Corb didn't say much of anything. He just kept right on to his business. I believe he did this because he knew that saying something to dad often just encouraged him to do it again. The second time dad sprayed Corb, this time a little heavier, Corb still did not say a word or even acknowledge that he had been wet. He just kept on working.

But the third time was a charm. When dad "accidentally" let the water go on Corb again, ol' Corb, without saying a word, just reached over with his razor sharp skinning knife and cut dad's brand new water hose clean in two. Then he went right on back to work, skinning the beef.

The look on my dad's face was priceless. He tried to think of something to say but was momentarily speechless. He just stood there with his mouth wide open. Finally, he said, "Damn you, Corb! You just cut my new water hose!" To which Corb dryly replied, "Yep." and just kept on skinning.

Well, as can be imagined, the rest of us who were working that day absolutely laughed until we cried. Not many times had any of us witnessed

Quincy Lee being the recipient of a practical joke like Corb had just put on him. After a couple of minutes, my dad was laughing as long and loud as the rest of us. He knew that Corb had gotten the best of him in that exchange. It was one time that I saw my dad lose in the practical joke wars, as least in the first round.

But, as was his custom, he came right back with his famous saying. "Corb,", he said, "You know damn well that is going to cost you." To which Corb responded, "Yep." and kept on skinning.

Chapter 28

SPLINTER UNDER DAD'S FINGERNAIL –
BE CAREFUL WHAT YOU ASK FOR!

My dad was a man of men through his adult life. He was a large man weighting over 300 pounds for most of his adult life. Not only was he large, he was a very strong man with forearms the size of most peoples legs and hands that looked as if they could crush whatever they were holding. And believe me, those hands had the strength of a vice-grip when he would grab a hold of you while horsing around or playing. He was tough as nails and had an extremely high tolerance for pain. He was also, to say the least, a little bit hard-headed, stubborn, and set in doing things his way. He was also a man that would, on occasion, O.K., more than on occasion, use a properly pronounced curse word, having been trained fully in the U.S. Navy. But, this combination of toughness, pain tolerance, and stubbornness led to one of the funnier stories that my mom loved to tell about my dad.

The story goes that dad and Uncle Homer, maybe a couple of other folks were working on the farm putting up fence. They were using old railroad cross ties as the corner fence post for this project. These posts sometimes weighed over 100 pound and were difficult to handle.

My dad was trying to put one of these posts down in the fence hole when the post slipped. Dad tried to grab it and when he did, a large splinter went up under his fingernail, almost to the first joint. Being the man that he was, he just pulled the large splinter out and kept on working. (Mistake Number 1)

Well, as he worked on the rest of the day, the wound under the fingernail began to hurt a little more and started to swell up. By the end of the day, it had swelled to the point that it was no longer open to drain fluid off and, within a few days, the wound became infected.

He tolerated this pain for a couple of more days and then he decided that it was not going to get any better without some type of remedy. Telling my mom about this and showing her the finger, he did not take her advice to go to the doctor or get some medicine for the ailment. (Mistake Number 2)

Instead, he told my mother, who was a registered nurse, that he had an idea of how to cure this finger. He asked her to get a hypodermic needle and syringe, fill it with methylate and slide it up under the nail using the same path made by the splinter, and then filling the entire area with said methylate as the needle was slowly extracted from under the finger nail.

Being the good nurse that she was, my mom warned my dad that this was not a good idea. In fact, she told him that this treatment would be so painful that he could not stand it. She told him that it would burn very badly and cause him to experience severe pain. But, again, being the tough, pain tolerant, hard headed, stubborn man that he was, my dad told my mom, "Woman, (he called her this in a very affectionate way when he wanted her to do something), just do what I am a' telling you to do. I know it may hurt a *little*, but it is hurting me so bad now that I can't hardly stand it. Every time my heart beats, I can feel it in my finger. It feels like a little boy is "buck" dancing on it." He did this while balling and un-balling his hand and making a motion like his heart was beating and he could feel it in his hand and finger with every beat of his heart. (Mistake Number 3)

After several attempts to get my dad to change his mind and finally seeing that there would be no way but dad's way (Mistake Number 4), she went and got the syringe, needle, and methylate. She filled the syringe full with an adequate amount of the orange liquid, attached the needle to the syringe, gently took dad by the hand and began the process of sliding the needle under the fingernail, all the way to the end of the channel that was made by the splinter a few days before.

As she started this minor operation, my dad, the tough, pain tolerant, hard headed, stubborn man that he was began to experience a little pain. He told my mom, as the needle entered, that it wasn't bad at all. She even reported that he made some comment about how she should have listened to him and what a good idea this had been.

But, things were about to change. As she started extracting the needle, filling the area under the fingernail with methylate as the needle was slowly pulled out, the pain started to, shall we say, intensify. As soon as the needle was completely removed and the area of the wound was fully exposed to the air, the pain began to increase.

It got hotter and hotter and hotter. Finally, my dad let loose of many choice words, to let my mom know how much his finger was now hurting. Then, according to my mom, my dad said, "Quick, Woman! Fill another one of them syringes full of that methylate and squirt it straight up my a__! That way I'll be able to catch myself because this damn finger is burning me so bad that I can't hardly stand it. I feel like I am going to take off running."

As you can imagine, my mom had the laugh of a life time with this. It was a classic moment for an "I told you so." between a husband and a wife. But, this time, it wasn't even necessary to say anything at all.

The end result of this little experimental medicine on my dad's finger was the infection went away in a couple of days and my dad's finger got better. But, he never did ask my mom to repeat this treatment on any future splinters. After all, even tough, pain tolerant, stubborn, hard headed men can learn from their mistakes.

Chapter 29

THE MEAT INSPECTOR

Have I mentioned in any of these essays that my dad was just the slightest bit hardheaded? Maybe just a tad on the stubborn side? Or that once in a while he would just lock down and not budge one inch from his chosen position on a matter. Well, the following story describes one of those times.

To fully understand this situation, one must know that my dad loved to process meat from the time he was a young man until he was unable to do so anymore because of health conditions. He loved to butcher his own beef and took great pride in being an expert at it. He could skin a beef, clean the carcass, divide it into quarters, hang them in the cooler for aging, and process the tripe.

Once properly aged, he could cut the beef up into the various cuts of meat with an experts touch. He knew how to cut T-bones, rib-eyes, round steak, flank steak, filet mignon, sirloins, and New York strips. He would grind the hamburger, make beef stew, prepare cubed steak, and beef ribs. Everyone who ever worked around him when he was processing a beef said he used everything but the moo.

It was the same with pork. He could do it all and many times we would process several hogs in one day. Again, he could butcher it, smoke it, cure the hams, make the bacon, cut the pork chops, fry the cracklings, and clean and eat the chitterlings all in one day. Over the next couple of days, he would make hog head cheese, made pork hash from the meat scraps, make the best pork sausage ever and either wrap it up in packages for pan sausage or stuff it in the casings for smoking as link sausage. As with the beef, dad would use everything but the oink on a hog when he was processing it.

Over the years of processing meat, many people came to dad and would buy meat from him or ask him to help them process their own meat. In particular, dad's sausage was loved by many people and it was not unusual for lots of folks to want to buy some of it when they would hear that he had made a fresh batch.

But, as with most good things in life, the government got involved in the meat processing business and wanted people to stop processing meat unless they followed all of the rules that had been set down for such activities. These rules especially prohibited the selling of meat from un-licensed or unregulated processors.

When these regulations were first put into practice, most of the state folks left people like my dad alone as long as they were discreet in the selling of meat to a few close friends or relatives. But, the longer the laws stayed in place and the more new inspectors that came on board, the more aggressive they became in trying to enforce the regulations.

One day, as dad was going about his business washing some vegetables from his garden, a young fellow came up and identified himself as a state meat inspector and tried to give my dad one of his business cards. My dad did not know the young fellow and instead of taking the card, he told the man that he could just lay it down over on the table as his hands were wet and he didn't want to take them out of the water until he was finished.

The young man did as dad said and then began to talk to my dad about some reports that he received from someone that my dad had been sell-ing meat without a license. He told my dad that he would have to stop butchering and processing the meat on his farm. As my dad had been in law enforcement for many years as a deputy, jail administrator and server of legal papers, he knew that it was not illegal for him to butcher and process meat for his own personal or family use, as long as he did not sell it.

With that knowledge, my dad just stopped what he was doing and said, "Young fellow. I am over 70 years old and I have been butchering my own meat on this farm all of my life. And, I intend to keep on doing it as long as I am able to do it." With that, he went back to washing the vegetables.

The state meat man just looked at my dad and decided to take a new approach. He said something like, "You are right Mr. Lee. You can butcher your own meat for your use but you can't sell any of it." My dad replied, "Yeah, I guess you are right. I am not supposed to sell it but I can give it to any damn body I want to give it to." Dad went on with his vegetable washing.

Once again, the young meat inspector tried a different approach. Instead of just telling dad about the rules and regulations, which he apparently had decided was not going to work, he then started to show dad the rules in written form. As he began to pull the papers out of a notebook he had with him to show to dad, my dad said, "You might as well put them papers back up. I can't read." Obviously, having graduated high school, spent four years in the navy, was a highly skilled master metal craftsman, as well as a meat expert, and had worked for many years in law enforcement, this was a total untruth. He could read anything he wanted to read. But, the young meat inspector could not prove this and therefore had no way to proceed with this line of trying to enforce the rules and regulations.

Now the meat inspector man was getting a little flustered with my dad. He then said something like, "Well, Mr. Lee, I am going to have to ask you to sign this paper here that says I have given you this information and that you understand it." My dad's reply was, "I've already told you that I can't read. And I ain't going to sign my name to something that ain't been read to me by someone I know and trust. Now if you want to stand there and read that to me, that'll be okay. But, I still ain't going to sign it because I don't know you."

Now the young fellow was completely perplexed. He could stand there and read the pages and pages of stuff to my dad, knowing that he was still not going to sign the paper saying that he understood the instructions to cease and desist in the selling of meat. Or, he could just leave the papers with my dad, with verbal instructions to cease and desist of selling meat, which was about a much use as the paper it was written on since he did not have dad's signature on any paper acknowledging his understanding of the rules and regulations. With that, he just told dad that he was leaving the papers for his information and went to his vehicle and left.

When dad finished washing the vegetables, he took the paper left by the meat inspector and tossed them into the burn barrel and set fire to them. The next time he made sausage, which was just a few weeks later, he sold it to any of his friends, relatives and fellow workers who wanted some. He kept on making and selling sausage over the last few years of his life just like he had been doing for 70 or more years. As far as I know, he never heard from or saw the young meat inspector again nor did he ever have contact again with anyone from the state meat inspector's office. I guess they decided it just wasn't worth the effort to deal with dad.

By the way, did I mention that dad was just a tad stubborn and hard-headed from time to time?

Chapter 30

TOP TEN LIST FOR COUNTRY FOLKS

On his late night television show each night, David Letterman reveals his nightly top ten list. These lists are usually made up of items from recent events that have been covered in the news, some sporting event or perhaps gleaned from various media sources in the entertainment industry. While watching one of these episodes, I decided to develop my own personal top ten list of things that many country folks get to experience or see that most city folks miss out on.

Before I reveal my top ten list, I understand these may not be applicable to all areas of the country. Some of the items on my list may be specific only in the Deep South or maybe only in the area of the country around northwest Florida, southeast Alabama, or southwest Georgia. Heck, some may even be confined to Holmes or Washington counties. But, if some of the items on my list don't apply to your own area, substitute others that may be just as good as mine because this is certainly not an exhaustive list. Just the ones that came to my mind at this time. So, here we go.

Top Ten for Country Folks

1. Watching the sun rise over Holmes Creek on an early, spring morning fishing for bream, shell crackers, stump knockers and other pan fish while the air is still crisp enough to be cool but warm enough to be comfortable in a boat with a good friend enjoying God's creation.

2. Walking behind a disk in a freshly plowed field in the spring barefooted, dressed only in a pair of cutoff jeans and drawers, feeling the coolness of the earth, smelling the aroma of the freshly tilled soil, watching the birds catch small bugs and worms that are being turned up as the tractor pulls the plow along, preparing the soil for a new crop of peanuts, corn, cotton, or watermelons.

3. Watching a pen full of drunk hogs after they have eaten corn soaked in fermented cane juice skimmings left over from making cane syrup. Quite a sight to see porkers on a binge with about 20 other drunk hogs! Sort of like going into a bar on a Saturday night with all of the same types of drunks – some fighters, some lovers, some happy, some mad and a few who just want to be left alone in their alcohol induced states of bliss.

4. Participating in a hog-killing weekend where those hogs that were drunk once upon a time in their lives make the ultimate sacrifice to provide homemade sausage, hams, pork chops, bacon and all of the other types of meat to be enjoyed by family and friends for the next several months.

5. Picking cotton (or tomatoes, corn, peas, butterbeans or any of several different crops) by hand for a full day in August when the sun beats down with a relentless fury, the rows are long, the cotton is thick and your mouth turns into a parched dust bowl and you can't drink enough water fast enough to replace the sweat pouring from you.

6. Going to or hosting a community wide, ya'll come and bring something to drink (your choice of course) southern peanut boil on a Saturday evening, listening to some good music, keeping up with a college football game or two, all the while sharing laughs and stories of life with good friends and loved ones.

7. Helping to make home-made pure cane syrup on a cold, clear late fall morning where the work starts early with the grinding of the cane and lasts into the late afternoon when the process has produced gallons and gallons of the tasty, amber colored syrup that is best when served with home-made biscuits, fresh pork sausage, some scrambled eggs, grits and gravy, and a big glass of cold milk.

8. Going to a southern family reunion where several generations of a family clan gather to celebrate life, share love, remember happy times, recall disappointments, show pictures of the new babies, and console those who have lost loved ones while eating oversized portions of the best food ever prepared by the loving hands of those in attendance.

9. Swimming in Holmes Creek on a steamy, hot Saturday afternoon in July when the air temperature is about 95 degrees and the crystal clear water of the spring fed stream is a constant 68 degrees which takes your breath away as you first dive into the water. The watermelons floating in the edge of the creek are getting cooler by the minute and will be consumed by all in attendance after about an hour of swimming while your body recovers some of the heat lost during the first swimming time. After the watermelons are eaten, the swimming starts again, ending only when all of the children are shaking life a leaf and their lips are a bright shade of blue from hypothermia caused by the cold creek water.

10. Going to a baptismal service early in the morning at the edge of this same Holmes Creek where some recently saved soul is

immersed in the cold water and into the family of believers while those in attendance sing "Amazing Grace" as the new convert emerges from the water to begin a new life in Christ.

Chapter 31

DEATH OF A LOCAL ICON

Davidavid Cook died today.

Though this event will go unnoticed and unnoted by the great majority of the world, it will be another mark on the calendar of time for those of us who lived in the Bethel Primitive Baptist Church/County Line Dirt Road community of Washington and Holmes counties in the Florida Panhandle. For you see, David Cook's small country grocery store was the point on the map through which our lives passed in many ways.

David Cook and his wife, Carolyn, owned and operated the little country store that was located on the corners of Highway 79 and Highway 280, later known as Douglas Ferry Road, in the northern part of Washington County, Florida, just below the Holmes County line. This little store was an important part of our entire community.

Early on in my life, the store was a simple, wooden building with a wood floor. David or Carolyn would be behind the counter, ready to ring up the sale or to point you to the proper place if you had a question about the location of an item. Later, the store was upgraded to a block building complete with large, plate glass windows in the front with a couple of aisles with real grocery store type shelves.

It was the place where most of the local people purchased the needed supplies to keep the many small family farms going. It was there that we bought the shelled corn and laying mash for the chickens, the hog pellets for the swine, the horse feed, the salt licking' blocks for the cows, and most any other kind of livestock feed required. It was the place that we purchased the various types of seed for the gardens that were to be planted each spring that signaled the beginnings of warm weather. But, this little store was much more than a place to purchase needed items.

This was also the place that we always stopped for an "RC cola and moon pie" as we were either headed to or were returning from an afternoon of swimming at a local swimming hole on Holmes Creek such as Cowford Landing, Burnt Sock Landing, Beckton Springs or down at the Vernon Park. The drinks were always cold and the moon pies sweet. It was the place that we stopped and got a cold drink between loads of hay going to the barn or some other type of farm labor. It was the place we bought some gas when we didn't want to go all the way to town.

At Cook's Store, we children could also buy those big ol' gingerbread cookies, pink punch drinks and chocolate drinks that were sort of like chocolate milk, only much sweeter. We could also purchase "candy cigarettes" complete in a lookalike Lucky Strike, Salem or Winston box. With these candy cigarettes, we could look all grown up, just like our moms and dads. Of course this was way before the days of political correctness and before the selling such items was outlawed.

Just an observation here but, my how times have changed in America. We outlaw the sale of candy cigarettes because it may entice youngsters to smoke. But, we protect the rights of people in the broadcast industry, such as television and movie makers, and the rights of people who send out filth over the internet, because it is their right to have freedom of speech. These people are constantly pushing for their "right" to broadcast whatever they wish over the public airways and into the homes across this land with millions of young boys and girls in them.

These programs often contain material that is, in my humble opinion, much more damaging to the children of America than a little candy that looks like a cigarette.

The response you get from these people is that parents can change the channel on the TV, turn the TV off, or put a block on the internet. I suppose these same brilliant folks, most of them liberals, didn't know that these same parents could have chosen not to buy the candy cigarettes if they were so concerned about their children learning to smoke from eating candy. By the way, I ate a bunch of candy cigarettes from Cook's Store and never was tempted to take up smoking as a habit.

Cook's Store was also the place where we would stop and purchase the required supplies for a day of fishing on the local waterways such as Holmes Creek, the Choctawhatchee River, or one of the numerous lakes in the area. It was almost a written rule that you had to stop at Cook's Store to buy the potted meat, Vienna sausage, crackers and sardines, cokes and other snacks that were necessary for a day of fishing. It was also the place that you just might find out where the fish were biting as you headed out.

This little store was an important part of the community information chain. You could stop in the store, hang around a little while and find out a whole lot about the happenings of the community. You could find out who was sick and who was getting better. You could hear about people who had moved away coming back home for family visits and who was going to see loved ones in distant places. You could find out about who was going to be having a hog killing, who had the first turnips ready in the garden and who had 'taters ready to dig in the spring. You could hear about weddings and births. And, yes, you could also hear about divorces and deaths.

This was not considered as gossip. It was just neighbors hearing about neighbors. It was friends hearing about friends. It was kinfolk keeping up with kinfolk. It was an important way for us to stay in touch with one another in the ebb and flow of life in our small, rural community.

Cook's Store was also the main geographical locator in the immediate area around the store. It was common knowledge around our area that any directions to get anywhere in or around there began with, "You go down 79 'til you get to Cook's Store and then turn......." For you see, the little store was located at the intersection of the two main paved roads in our area. From this intersection, you could go to Bonifay (north), Vernon (south), Hinson's Crossroads (southwest), Chipley (northeast), or Caryville (south, then west). You could begin there to go the river or creek, find homes on unmarked dirt roads and any of the several local churches.

For example, giving directions to someone's house might go something like this- "Well, let's see now. You go on down there to Cook's Store and turn right. You then need to go about 4 or 5 miles and you will come to Five Points. You keep on going past there for about another mile or so. Then, if you will start to look on your left, you will see a dirt driveway that leads up a little hill. It will be a clay driveway. That is where you turn and the white, frame house right up there on the left will be Preacher Todd's. Now, if you miss it and go too far, you will find an intersection of the Caryville and Vernon Highway. If you get that far, turn around. If you don't find it, heck, then just stop and ask some of the folks around there. They will tell you how to get there."

Cook's Store closed a few years ago. David and Carolyn were approaching the age that we will all reach at some time, if we are so blessed, when it was time to slow down and retire. But, when the store closed, for many of us, it was like another chapter in the book of life being closed. It was another signal to our community that life keeps moving on and, as the country song says, the only thing that stays the same is the fact that things keep changing.

I believe that I can safely speak for most of the people who lived in our community in years past by saying that I am glad to have the memories of Cook's Store in my mind. I am glad that I knew David Cook, Carolyn and their family. I am pleased to have had the opportunity to buy an "RC cola and moon pie" at Cook's Store after an afternoon of swimming in Holmes Creek. And, though most of the entire world will not mourn the passing of David Cook, I will. So will many others who lived in our community. After all, a local icon that helped to define the lives of myself and many others has passed.

Chapter 32

JURY DUTY – HOLMES COUNTY STYLE

Being called for or summonsed for jury duty is one of those civic duties that most people do not enjoy. I don't believe that I have ever heard anyone say, "Boy, I hope they select me for jury duty for the next session of circuit court!" Most people look upon this civic responsibility with some sense of dread and it is common for many to think of creative ways to avoid this duty. But, one time several years ago, I was glad that I had been selected for duty. This opportunity for fulfilling my civic duty provided me with a lasting memory as I got to witness a hilarious episode of jury selection, Holmes County style.

The jury selection process started in a normal manner with the members of the jury pool seated out in the courtroom waiting for the judge to come into the courtroom. The judge for this particular case to be heard was the Honorable Judge John Roberts, a veteran circuit court judge in our area. Upon entering the courtroom, he began the process of questioning potential jurors of their worthiness to serve on the jury panel.

He started this process by asking the potential jurors if they were all citizens of Holmes County. This is when the fun began. One fellow who was a member of the jury pool shouted out in a pretty loud manner,

"Yep, Judge, I have lived in Holmes County my whole life." At this, Judge Roberts just looked at the man with a shake of his head but said nothing.

The next question Judge Roberts asked was, "Are all members of the jury pool registered voters?" This question was necessary because of how jury pool members are selected. Again, the ol' boy up front just hollered out in the courtroom, "Yes sir, Judge, I have voted in every election since I turned eighteen!"

Now this person in the jury pool was a red-neck seeming sort of fellow. He was dressed in a blue Duck-head work shirt with matching blue Duck-head pants, a cap with a blue bill in his hand and work boots on his feet. The clothes were clean but looked as if they had been saved for this special occasion in court. You could also tell from his outbursts in the court that his language was pure north Florida country with a slow drawl.

At this second outburst in the courtroom, Judge Roberts said to the man, "Sir, please do not shout out in the courtroom anymore. It is not proper courtroom decorum." The man answered with a very firm, out loud, "Yes, Sir!" Again, Judge Roberts just looked at him over his glasses and shook his head.

The next question from Judge Roberts was, "Has anyone here ever been convicted of a crime before?" The man asked out loud, "Judge, does a speeding ticket count?" At this, Judge Roberts very firmly said, "No, Sir. A speeding ticket does not count. But, one more time, please do not shout out into the courtroom anymore. If you have a question, raise your hand and I will send a bailiff to answer your question. If the answer to any question is yes, just nod your head. If it is no, just shake your head. Do you understand?" Again, the man answered, "Yes, Sir." in a pretty loud voice.

The next question asked by Judge Roberts was, "Do any of you know anything about the case that is to be tried here this morning?" At this, the ol' boy once again just shouted out into the courtroom, "I ain't never heard nothin' about this case. I don't even read the paper very much."

At this, Judge Roberts took his glasses off, laid them on the desk in front of him, pointed at the man, motioned with his fingers and said, "Come here!" The man started towards the bench. Upon arrival, Judge Roberts started to talk to him. He said, "I thought I told you to ..." and he just stopped in mid-sentence. He looked down at the man and said, in a very animated, strong voice, "Have you been drinking?"

The ol' boy looked up at Judge Roberts and said, "Now, Judge, I had one beer (while holding up one finger) before I came over here this morning, but I ain't drunk!" To this, Judge Roberts said, "Bailiff, take this man for a breathalyzer right now!" The bailiff hauled the man out of the courtroom and we did not see him anymore. I guess they found that he had had more than one beer on the way to court.

It was all I could do not to laugh out loud in the court as to the developments of the morning. I could not believe that some knot head had pulled such a stunt when called to serve on jury duty. It was another one of those moments that could only happen in Holmes County. I guess this fellow could be the answer to a Jeff Foxworthy quotation, "You might just be a red-neck if you have ever been arrested for being drunk while you were getting ready to be a part of the jury pool."

Chapter 33

ROOT CANAL

If you have never had a root canal, stop reading right here. There is no need for you to have recurrent anxiety about the possibility that you may need to have a root canal in the future. It just wouldn't be worth it to read any further.

For those of you who have had a root canal, I hope that your experience was a pleasant one. After all, I am quite sure that there are root canals performed in America where you do not end up traumatized for life. There are most likely root canals done every day that are almost painless. But, my first one, probably my only one unless I go senile, was a little bit of a challenge. Please allow me to share this experience with you.

It was a normal dental appointment with my good friend and dentist, Dr. Jeff "I would use an ice pick and hand drill if I could" Swindle. The particular tooth that was the reason for the visit had been giving me a little problem for some time, and the good doctor had tried a couple of other remedies over the past few weeks. When it continued to cause me pain, he said those famous words, "Well, the only other option that I know is to either pull it or do a root canal on it."

Now I knew several people who had had root canals. These people survived with no apparent long-lasting consequences, though I had noticed a couple of them did have a little head twitch and broke out in cold sweats at the mention of going to a dentist. How was I to know that this was caused by their own memories of having had a root canal?

I decided that I would have the root canal. It seemed like a logical, well thought out decision at the time. I did not want to lose the tooth since it was sort of in the middle of my lower jaw and pulling it would have required a partial plate to be inserted. Because I had seen my dad's partial plate grow over the years from one tooth to an almost full set of false teeth, I did not want to start down that road at the age of about 40.

Besides all that, I have also seen the pliers used by dentist to remove teeth. They look a whole lot like the pliers we used on the family farm when I was growing up to work on trucks and tractors. I really didn't want a pair of those pliers anywhere near my teeth or mouth. So the appointment was made to start the root canal.

A few days later, I returned to Dr. Jeff, "The Sadist" Swindle to begin the process. It began with little warning of the excitement to come. I found out that a root canal is not a "one visit to the dentist and you are done" procedure. It requires at least a couple of visits, maybe more, depending upon the particular tooth being worked on. He began to drill out the area of the tooth necessary to do work. I believe I remember that he had a little smile on his face when he began to work on my tooth. I wondered why?

He put in a "temporary filling" in preparation for the next visit when the actual root canal would begin. For those who may not know, the root canal procedure is one in which the nerves in the tooth are actually removed. This process, in simple layman's terms, involves drilling into the tooth, using some type of medicine to cause the nerves in the tooth to go numb and then employing a small instrument that looks somewhat like a miniature crochet hook to remove these nerves. No nerves left in the tooth, no pain left in the tooth. Sounds simple, huh?

On my second visit of this process, Dr. Jeff "This is gonna be fun!" Swindle began to do the things necessary to remove the nerves from the tooth. He began by giving me the normal shot of Novocain or whatever it is that dentists use to numb the mouth before drilling out the temporary filling. He then did whatever dentist do to deaden the nerves way down in the tooth. I need to mention here that it *is really, really* important for all of these nerves way down in the tooth to be deadened.

Otherwise, pain. Not a little pain. Not just sort of a little twitch in your mouth pain. Not just a small grunt of pain. Not even a pain like childbirth, though being a male I have never had a child, though the pain of childbirth could not be much different. I am talking about P-A-I-N!

Anatomically speaking, teeth have different numbers of roots in them. Some near the front of the mouth have one root. Others further back in the mouth have two, three or more roots. This particular tooth was *supposed* to have three canals that had nerves in them. In a root canal, the dentist is supposed to go into each of these canals down deep in the tooth and remove the nerves one at the time until all are gone. Then the dentist can re-fill the tooth, and the tooth should now be pain free.

However, on this particular tooth of mine, there were four canals that contained nerves, not three. Dr. Jeff, "Dang, I didn't know there were four canals on that one." Swindle was using his miniature crochet hook, going up and down in the canals in the tooth, to remove the nerves.

Then it happened. He stuck that dad-blamed, cuss-fired, full-sized (or so it felt) crochet hook down into canal number four. The one that he didn't know was there. ***The one that he had not deadened.***

The pain told my brain that the crochet hook instrument had stopped just short of some other fairly delicate parts of the human anatomy!! In fact, it felt like he was just inches from performing some other delicate type of surgery, like a vasectomy, on me.

I am not sure how he knew that something had just caused great pain in my body. Maybe it was because of the wild look in my eyes. Maybe it was because I was trying my best to imitate my dad, who has been known to use the occasional curse word or two, though this was not possible because the doctor's hands were in my mouth so I couldn't speak. I am pretty sure that I did try to bite him.

In really considering how he knew that I was in pain, I believe that I now remember how he was able to determine this. It was because I was very suddenly about three feet up in the air, out of the chair, having levitated there by the very quick, extremely tight contraction of my butt muscles when he stuck that dad-blamed, cuss-fired, full-sized crochet hook into that canal in the tooth that had not been deadened.

Being a former coach and having some knowledge of muscle ability and performance capabilities, I did not know until this moment that your butt muscles could cause a person lying in a perfectly supine position to rise into the air like the great magician Houdini without moving another muscle. But, believe me, it is possible.

I don't remember how long I was up in the air that day. Maybe a few seconds; maybe just a split second; maybe until Dr. Jeff "Dang, did you all see that?" Swindle, pushed me gently back into the dental chair to finish the procedure. I do remember that it was pain that caused this spontaneous performance of levitation.

After this, Dr Jeff "I believe that I will now deaden that last nerve" Swindle apologized and gave me another shot of Novocain. When it took effect, he completed the procedure. I am happy to report that the tooth now gives me no problems at all. In retrospect, I suppose it was worth it.

A few days ago, I went back to Dr. Jeff "Well, I'll be! After that last root canal, I can't believe you are back." Swindle. He filled a tooth for me that had been giving me a little pain. With just the hint of a smile on his face, he said something about if this doesn't work, we may have to do a root canal on it.

I broke out in a cold sweat. A little shiver ran down my spine. Had a quick, almost unnoticeable twitch in my head.

I left his office and went to the hardware store. Bought myself a nice, new pair of pliers.

Chapter 34

UNCLE JOHN D. GETS A NEW TRUCK

My Uncle John D. Lee bought himself a new truck last Thursday, June 15, 2006. I realize this does not sound like a big deal since lots of people buy new trucks or cars every day. But, this was a very big deal for Uncle John D.

You see, Uncle John D., my dad's older brother, just bought himself the very first new vehicle of any kind that he has ever owned. He paid cash for a brand new, candy apple red Chevrolet Silverado truck. He is 93 years young.

Some background information for a fuller understanding about this happening will probably be helpful. There were five children in my dad's family, two girls and three boys. They were Ruby, who died at age 95; Janie, who died at 93; Homer, who died at 88; Uncle John D., who is still pretty spry for a man of 93 and my dad, who is presently 85. I suppose this was a pretty strong bloodline since the youngest of my dad's siblings died at 88 while all of the others lived into their 90's.

Uncle John D., like all of the rest, was raised on the family farm that was homesteaded by my grandfather and grandmother, Silas D. Lee and Mary Della Brock Lee. The family was very typical of the other families around the Bethel Church community of the early 1900's- poor but proud, largely uneducated, hard working people who lived off the land. As a matter of fact, my dad is the only one of the family that graduated from high school.

Uncle John D. grew up in this environment and went to work just like all the rest of the family, doing whatever he could do to earn a living in the early years of his adult life. He did a little of everything including farming, logging, making and selling moonshine to earn a living for him and his family.

He was always a thin, small framed man who looked like he would not weigh over 100 pounds, soaking wet. I remember as a child I would wonder how he could be so small and my dad be so large, weighing close to 300 pounds and a hulk of a man, and be brothers. We used to accuse dad of being the baby of the family and getting all of the best food and Uncle John D. just getting the leftovers was what made one so big and the other so small. I also remember how much Uncle John D. looked like my paternal grandfather.

Anyway, one of the jobs that he tried as a means of earning a living was building roads. It was in this capacity that he found a job that he liked. He ended up working for the Washington County Road Department for over 30 years, mainly as a heavy equipment operator, mostly running a road grader. This was at a time when Washington County had hundreds of miles of dirt roads that required grading on a regular basis to keep them passable.

All during this time, the wages that he earned were not enough to allow him to own a new vehicle, especially when raising a family with three children and a stay at home housewife. I can still see him coming to visit my grandparents or parents, driving some old beat up truck that he had obtained from some acquaintance, friend or neighbor. These old vehicles were often collections of odd colors, spare parts from other vehicles and held together with nuts, bolts, and hay bailing wire. It was always a question of whether or not they would crank up and leave for the return trips home.

As he aged, he still collected vehicles from various sources to meet his transportation needs. The latest of these came from a neighbor who had become very ill and could no longer drive. Uncle John D. drove this old truck for several years. However, it left him stranded by the road on more than one occasion.

Finally, the old hand-me-down truck reached the end of the road. Uncle John D. decided that it was time for different transportation. First, he had my brother-in-law, Wayne Johnson, who has been his unofficial caretaker for the last few years, to drive him to a car dealership in Marianna. Uncle John D. was once again looking for a used truck. But, upon pricing some of the used trucks, Wayne convinced him that he could buy a brand new truck cheaper than the used ones. So, they went to another dealership in DeFuniak Springs and began to bargain with the salesman. Before long, they had a deal.

Uncle John D. was going to get a brand new truck. They even offered to finance it for him, which I find pretty funny. After all, offering to finance a truck for five years to a 93 year old man seems to me to have a pretty significant amount of risk tied to it. But, he didn't want any of that. He paid them with a check for the new truck and drove it home. What a great day for him!

We had a big family dinner for Father's Day on June 18, 2006 at my dad's house and Uncle John D. drove his new truck to the gathering. We all had to see the new truck and even took several pictures of him with the new truck. He was smiling like a mule eating briars through a barbed wire fence.

Pretty amazing, this new truck purchase. Amazing that it is the first new vehicle of any kind that Uncle John D. has ever owned. Amazing that he is still in good enough health to drive. Amazing that even at his age, a new truck was just like a new toy to him with all of the excitement and joy that such a purchase would bring to anyone.

No, that's not correct. More excitement and joy than it would bring to almost anyone else. I believe, after 93 years, he has earned the right to be as excited and happy as he wants to be.

Chapter 35

KAMI GIVES VASELINE A NEW NAME

A few days ago, my oldest daughter, Ashley, called and asked if my wife could pick up our 3 year old granddaughter, Kami, because she had a "tummy ache" along with a little case of diarrhea. Being the loving grandmother, my wife went to get her immediately.

On the ride home, Kami told my wife that she needed to use the rest room "real bad because my tummy is hurting." As they got closer to the house, Kami began to cry a little and was telling my wife that she did not think that she could hold it. But, my wife was telling her to try real hard because they were almost home.

When they arrived at the house, Kami had been successful in not having an accident. But, she told Nana Lee again that she was "about to go pooh-pooh" in her panties. My wife told her to take off and run to the rest room. But, just as Kami was going through the living room to the rest room, the accident happened. She began to cry again, saying she had messed up her pants.

But, once again, my wife calmed her down and told her it was okay and that every little boy or girl had an accident once in a while. She told her to go ahead to the rest room and climb over into the tub and she would just give her a quick bath after she had cleaned her up. This seemed to satisfy Kami as she stopped crying and headed on to the rest room. She got into the tub, my wife helped her get out of the messed up clothing, cleaned her up and ran her some bath water.

After she had finished bathing, Kami got out of the tub and was letting her Nana dry her off. During the drying off process, Nana noticed that Kami had some irritation on her little rear end as a result of having had the diarrhea. My wife told her to stand still and she was going to get some Vaseline to put on her butt and that it would help her to feel better.

My wife went to get the Vaseline and when she got back, she had Kami lean over the side of the tub so she could treat the affected area. She gently swabbed the irritated area with the Vaseline on a cotton swab and as this was going on, my granddaughter looker around at her and said in her best little southern, country voice that is her natural way of speaking, *"Soo, Nana Lee, is that the reason that they call that stuff Ass-e-Line?"*

After almost choking to keep back the laughter, my wife tried to explain to Kami that the name of the ointment was Vaseline, making sure that she understood that the word started with a "V" sound. But, she could not wait to tell me and others about the new name that Kami had given to this valuable commodity.

In thinking about this, I bet that a lot of people would think this is a perfectly good name for this product. I myself can attest to the cooling and healing power of the product in certain cases of bodily distress over the years, especially in some rather sensitive locations.

Anyway, Kami gave my wife a great laugh on that day. It is one of those things that kids can say at any time that build lasting memories and make life worth living.

Chapter 36

FIRST DAY OF SCHOOL

Today is August 18, 2008.

It is the first day of school for 2008 and my beautiful twin daughters, Abby and Anna, are getting ready to go to school. Big Seniors! Members of the Ruling Class at Holmes County High School!

As I walk by the refrigerator getting ready for breakfast, a photo on the door catches my eye. It is a picture of Abby. She is a little girl in the picture, not the young lady that she is now. She is dressed in a brightly colored outfit, hair in a pony tail, and smiling from ear-to-ear. The picture is in a paper holder with a small magnet that holds it to the refrigerator. The caption on the holder reads "My First Day in First Grade."

Where did the time go? That picture on the refrigerator was taken yesterday, or so it seems in my mind. How did "the girls," as their mom and I often refer to them, get this old, this fast? When did they finish elementary school or middle school? When did they change from the little girls in the picture to the young ladies they are now? How fast it seems to me. How slow it may have seemed to them.

These last eleven years have been a blur in time. It seems to have passed at the speed of light. So much has happened, but it seems as if it all took place in a day, maybe a week, or, at most, in a month.

Since the picture was taken, here are a few of life's happenings that have taken place.

We have had three or four new refrigerators. The picture has made the trip every time.

There have been piano lessons, though these did not result in the development of much musical skill, due to a lack of practice. However, both girls love music, so maybe the lessons weren't a total waste.

We have built a new home and moved two times. The new house has seen the change in Abby and Anna from little girls to young women. It has also been home to several pets, including dogs Watson and Buddy, some rabbits, a couple of cats. The latest addition is GiGi, the Wal-Mart parking lot dog that was brought home by Anna and her mom after a trip to the store that now rules the house with her personality.

Our family has lost three of the children's grandparents, including both my mom and dad and Mike's mom. These were tough times for all of us to bear. But, we have also had two new additions, with the birth of our first two grandchildren, who belong to our oldest daughter, Ashley.

The girls have participated in many activities, including church league basketball, youth group activities, and school organizations. They have been cheerleaders for six years and are now captains of the varsity squad. Many memories will be carried through life from these activities.

Driver's licenses have been obtained. There have been several minor accidents, a couple of fender benders, and one serious accident in which Abby totaled the car she was driving. Only by the grace of God was she here to start her senior year in high school. Thank God for miracles, protection, and for letting us keep our beautiful daughter.

There have been more boyfriends than I care to count and a group of girl friends that have been close to each other since their first days in school. Some of these relationships will probably be life-long though others will fade, *with time.*

I could go on and on about the happenings during the last few years. But, that would turn into a much more lengthy literary work than is intended here. But, the time from the beginning of first grade to the beginning of the 12th grade does warrant further consideration.

I suppose it is a mystery worthy of men much smarter than I to try and explain the compression of time as we get older. Why does tomorrow seem like forever to a child waiting on Christmas when that same time arrives quickly for older people? After all, the days contain some 23 hours, 56 minutes, and a few seconds for both the young and the old. But, the time seems to pass at different rates.

I can remember as a child my mom used to tell a story about my waking up and telling her that I was *finally* seven years old. I must have been waiting anxiously for that birthday. But, now I can barely recall when the twins were seven, or eight, nine, or ten for that matter. I now go back and look at other photographs of the three children, and it is as if they have literally jumped from small children to young adults. This metamorphosis of changing from child to adult has happened much quicker than a butterfly develops from a caterpillar.

However, to the girls, I would bet the times have moved somewhat slower. They can recall many more details about these years than I could ever remember. They are busy building memories, storing these into their own life remembrances. The times are still moving somewhat slowly for them. But somewhere between now and mid-life, this will change for them also, though I don't know how to warn them about this. I can't even tell them when this passing of time changed from slow to fast for me.

Many books have been written which try to explain the essence of time. Albert Einstein spent a great portion of his life in the study of time. The Bible has many passages that relate to time historically and philosophically, making predictions about the future and detailing events of the past. The book of Ecclesiastes speaks a great deal about time including passages about a time to live, a time to sew, a time to reap, and a time to die.

As for me, the time from the first day in first grade to the first day in twelfth grade for Abby and Anna has passed much too quickly. I wish that I could capture some of it, call it back. I wish the time had not passed so fast. It is a selfish wish only for me.

Chapter 37

TWO BULLS BUTT HEADS

On a cattle ranch, it is not unusual to witness two bulls in a battle of wills to determine which of the bulls will be the "top dog" among a herd of cows. These battles sometimes last for a good while and are punctuated with pawing at the ground, throwing dust in the air, bellowing and snorting, and other displays of anger. The story below details one such battle between an old bull and a younger bull in our family. In order for the reader to fully understand this battle of wills, some background information is provided in the next few paragraphs.

After my mom passed away, it fell upon my sister Janis and me to try, (I say "try") to manage the health affairs of our dad, Quincy Lee. My brother Silas would have done some of this, but he did not live close to Dad, and he was not as comfortable in dealing with the health care professionals as Janis and I were. Now, this may not seem like a big deal to most folks, but to say there were challenges associated in doing this would be an understatement. There were probably several reasons for this.

One of these was that my mother had been a nurse for all of the years that Mom and Dad were married, and she was always the one to guide him in his dealings with health- related issues. She made the doctor's appointments, got the medicine, handled the paperwork, paid the bills, and talked to the insurance folks. So, when she passed away before him, he was not really all that familiar with the processes. Some of the health issues that we had to deal with on a regular basis were several heart-related problems (high blood pressure, atrial fibrillation), skin cancer, arthritis (two knee replacements) and obesity. However, since he had had these health issues for a number of years, he was familiar with the doctors he liked, the ones he didn't like, knew a good deal about his medications, and was convinced he didn't need our help. So, problem number one was an uncooperative patient.

Problem number two was that fact that my dad was an independent, self-reliant, head-strong, hard-headed man who did not like it one little bit for his children to be telling him what he needed to do. After all, he had been telling them what to do for the last 55 years or so and did not seem to have any inclination toward having these roles reversed. So, he was not real happy to have two of his children telling him which doctors he needed to see, making doctor's appointments for him, taking him to these appointments, going in with him to ask questions of the doctors, and making decisions about his health care based on this information. As a means of expressing his displeasure, he started calling us "Dr. Johnson" and "Dr. Lee" to anyone who would listen to him complain about our meddling in his business.

Perhaps the greatest hindrance to us lending assistance to dad in his health care was that he also hated going to the doctor unless absolutely necessary and his definition of necessary was somewhat different than ours. We made sure that he had routine checkups for all of the issues that we knew about, and he considered these appointments as a waste of time for the most part. Once in a while, he wouldn't fuss too much about an appointment with his heart doctor, but other than that, he resisted going.

The fact that dad had two knee replacements was always a matter that required monitoring because at any time there was a danger of his getting some type of infection that would end up having an impact on the artificial joints. The doctors had told him several times that any infection reaching the knee joints would have the potential to cause him either to have another knee replacement, which was not a good prospect because of his age and size, or to have the affected leg removed from the knee down.

Now, with this information, the story of two bulls butting heads begins.

Dad had been feeling bad for a couple of days and we had been checking on him as usual. Janis had even mentioned that he might need to see the doctor because it appeared that he was coming down with some type of severe cold, flu, or respiratory infection. But he kept on telling us that he was not going to the doctor, that he was okay and for us to leave him alone. He would let us know if he needed to go to the doctor. Yeah, right!!!

Anyway, I was at work and Janis was at a meeting of some type when I received a call from the lady who cleaned Dad's house for him. She said that I probably should come and check on him as he was really not feeling good and had told her that he had been up several times during the night sick to his stomach. She also reported he was also running a fever and had not even gotten dressed that morning and it was close to 10:00. So, I immediately left work and went to check on Dad.

When I got to his home, he was still sitting in his recliner dressed only in his underwear and undershirt. After a short conversation, I told him he really needed to go to the doctor. Of course, I got his standard answer, "I don't need to go to the doctor. I'll be all right." Well, I could see this was going to be fun, because I had made up my mind that I wasn't leaving until he agreed to go.

This is about when the two bulls, the old one and the younger one from the same herd, started butting heads complete with pawing at the ground, snorting, and bellowing.

I started out trying to reason with him about why he needed to see a doctor. His response was that he wasn't going to the doctor because he could just get some medicine called in to the drugstore. I looked at his legs and could see they were very red below the knee and looked as if an infection was setting in, close to the artificial knees.

Seeing this, I told him, "Dad, you are going to have to go to the doctor. They need to see these legs and get you started on antibiotics."

"I ain't going to the doctor. Maybe tomorrow."

"No, tomorrow may be too late. You are going today."

"Now, Bill, I believe that I can make my own decisions—and I ain't going!"

"Dad, you are dang sure going to go to the doctor today!"

"No, I am not going to the doctor today!"

These exchanges continued for several minutes, with each bull pawing at the ground, snorting at each other more with each exchange, voices bellowing louder and louder, until finally the old bull said, "No, I damn sure ain't going to the doctor!"

The younger bull then replied, ***"Dad, you know that I love you and I don't want to talk to you like this. But, you damn sure are going to go to the doctor today. Now, you can get dressed and go with me or I am going to call the ambulance and tell them to bring whatever they have to bring with them to load your fat ass up on a stretcher and take you to the hospital. But, one way or the other, you are damn sure going."***

Dad's replay was once again a matter-of-fact statement that he wasn't going. My reply to that was to pick up the telephone and start to dial. When he asked what I was doing, I told him I was calling Janis to tell her what was going on and then calling the ambulance for them to come and get him. I also told him that Janis was on the way too and that if he thought I had been giving him "hell," he hadn't heard anything yet. At this, he finally said that if I would just leave him alone for a few minutes, he reckoned he would get up, put some clothes on, and go with me.

After a short delay, the lady who had called me and witnessed this exchange brought dad some clean clothes, and we got him dressed. I helped him to my vehicle and we headed out to the doctor. Also at the house that day was a close friend of Dad's who had been trying to get him to agree to go to a doctor before I had arrived. When the two bulls started butting heads, he just went off to another corner of the corral and watched. But, when Dad and I were heading out toward the vehicle, he took hold of my arm and, laughing, said he had just witnessed a battle between an old bull and a younger bull and was glad the younger bull won.

We went directly to the hospital in Panama City because of the issues with the leg, the infection, and the cold/flu symptoms. The diagnosis—dad had a severe infection in his chest, close to pneumonia, and in the legs. The doctor told us had we waited another day, he would have had no choice but to either operate on the leg that was the most infected and try to save the artificial knee or either remove the leg from above the knee down. During this visit, it was also determined that dad was diabetic (unknown before this hospital stay) and was started on new medicines to address this new health issue.

By the way, this little hospital stay only lasted six days! Good thing he really didn't need to go to the doctor!!!

I wish I could report that Dad became more cooperative after this and was not as resistant to Janis's and my help with his medical needs. Not even close. If anything, he became worse. He steadfastly refused to acknowledge that he was diabetic and resisted any attempts to modify his diet and check his blood sugar levels. Because of this new diagnosis, he also had to start seeing a new doctor who specialized in treatment of diabetes. He absolutely hated to go to this new doctor and raised a fuss about it with every appointment. There were several more opportunities for the two bulls (or one old bull and one cow) to butt heads over medical issues.

Up until his passing, Dad did not come to like his children telling him what to do. He did not modify his resistance to going to see doctors. He certainly did not become any less hard-headed, independent, and headstrong.

I guess the only good thing about this was the fact that the young bull and cow that he was dealing with were from the same brood stock and were pretty comfortable in barnyard battles.

Chapter 38

ONE MORE STEAK

I don't believe that there has ever been a man who loved a rare, grilled T-Bone or Rib-eye steak better than my dad. He loved his steaks very rare, just a little brown on each side and warm in the middle. This was without a doubt his favorite meal with a baked potato and salad.

But, a few months back, he had a light stroke. This has made it difficult for him to chew and swallow certain foods because of a very slight impairment in his throat. Some of the food he wants to eat makes him cough and almost chokes him. So, now all of his food has to be pureed (ground up) with a food processor in order for him to eat it. He has also lost weight to the point that his false teeth no longer fit properly so he can't chew anything at all.

It is difficult for me to watch him in his hospital bed and in the nursing home where he has been since the stroke trying to eat this chopped up food. He struggles a little getting the food up to his mouth and nothing tastes good to him all mixed together. He tells me and anyone else who will listen how bad the food is and how he wishes he could get something good to eat.

Because of the effects of the stroke, dad is in physical therapy every day, trying to get strong enough to one day leave the nursing home and go back to his home. He is making slow progress toward this goal, getting a little more able each day to do the routine things necessary to be able to go home such as get in and out of his wheelchair, the bed and go to the restroom.

I only wish that he could make progress to the point that he is not only able to go home, but to get him some new false teeth that fit so that he can eat real food again. If that ever happens, I am going to the local butcher shop, buy the best piece of prime, tender beef they have, go home, grill it rare, and serve it to my dad.

I want to see that look of pure enjoyment in his eyes one more time when he takes a bite of his favorite meal.

Chapter 39

THE BURYING SUIT

My dad was not one of those men who felt the need to own several suits so he could choose the one he was planning to wear based on the occasion. To the best of my memory, he owned only one suit at the time and wore a suit only when absolutely necessary, preferring instead to wear a pair of slacks and a white short-sleeved shirt for all but the dressiest events. If he were required to be in a suit, it was because someone had passed away, was getting married or maybe celebrating a very special occasion such as a 50th wedding anniversary. Other than times like these, he was rarely caught in a suit.

Because of this, he tended to keep any suit that he owned for long periods of time, only getting a new one if he outgrew the old one or if it became so old and worn that it required replacing. It was at one of these times when the old suit had to go that our family got a lasting memory of life with Quincy Lee.

This event started when my mom, my sister Janis, and I began a discussion about dad needing a new suit. The old suit that he had at the time was one that he had worn for about 10 or more years. It was light gray in color, looking much like the suits that Andy Griffin wore on the television show "Matlock." The old suit had a few bare spots on the coat and pants and more than one stain or spot visible. It was definitely time for dad to upgrade his wardrobe with a new suit.

My sister and mom set about trying to find and buy this new suit for dad. It was not easy to find a suit that would fit him because he was a large man who required a coat that was about a size 50 in the chest and pants that had to be adjusted to fit his height and waist. After some effort and searching, they finally found a suit they loved and purchased it. We decided to give this suit to dad as a part of his Christmas from the family.

Christmas times at Mom and Dad's were always special events. All of the children and grandchildren would gather out at the home place on Christmas day. We would all arrive in time to help prepare and eat the noontime dinner meal. These meals were true family feasts complete with turkey and dressing, giblet gravy, cranberry sauce, cream corn, peas or butterbeans, turnip greens, mustard greens, baked ham, corn bread, rolls, and several kinds of desserts. Dad always sat at the head of the table and gave directions about who was to say the blessing and instructions about passing the food. Most of the time, no one paid much attention to him on this day as the food would move up and down the table with each person dipping the desired portion on his or her plate. It would be safe to say that we were all guilty of gluttony during these Christmas dinners.

After dinner, the dining room and kitchen would be cleaned up while all of the children (and most of the men) would start making their way to the living room eager to get started opening the presents that were under the tree. This was always a time of great excitement as the children could hardly wait to tear into the gifts with their names on them.

The tradition in our family was that the grandchildren who were old enough to read the names on the packages would hand out the gifts to all of those present. This started when my twin nephews, Brad and Chris, and my niece Linda, were old enough to hand out the presents. When they got a little older, they passed this duty down to another nephew,

Jared, and my oldest daughter, Ashley. When it was time for them to move aside, my twin daughters Abby and Anna took over.

The gifts would be handed out to everyone and all would begin opening their gifts immediately, except for my dad. He would hold all of his gifts in a pile and wait until everyone else had finished. Then he would delay some more until all of the grandkids would go over to him, plead with him to start opening his presents, watch him as he stalled some more, and then begin to lend him a hand with his presents. It was the same show every year. It was just his way of enjoying Christmas with the grandkids.

Anyway, on this particular Christmas, the gifts had all been passed out and we all waited for Dad to begin opening his presents. He finally finished opening all of the ones that had been handed to him. Then, my sister went and got one more present for him to open.

It was a large box, neatly wrapped with pretty paper. Janis insisted that he open this present himself. Well, after the expected delay tactics and much coaxing for him to open the gift, he did so. When he pulled the top off the box, inside was a beautiful Navy blue suit with very fine white pin-stripes running vertically down the jacket and pants. It was a very fine-looking suit that anyone would have been proud to own and wear.

But, my dad took one look at the new suit and declared, "I ain't wearing that damn suit. You might as well take it back." Well, that certainly wasn't what we were expecting to hear. My sister was shocked. She got up and went over to where he was sitting and began to talk with him about the suit. She took the coat up out of the box, held it up and began to tell him how pretty it was. Mom also began to tell him it was a beautiful suit and started talking to him about how much time they had spent looking for it and making sure it was the right size. All the while they were asking him why he would not wear the suit—with no response from Dad.

They might as well have been talking to the King of England in Spanish. In other words, it wasn't doing any good. He just sat there, telling them over and over that he wasn't going to wear it. Finally, my sister said to him, "Well, will you at least try it on?" To which he replied, "I damn sure ain't going to wear it or even try it on!" Reaching a point of exasperation, my sister asked one more time, "Why won't you wear the suit?"

My dad's reply has become a family classic—"Because it looks like a damn burying suit! And I ain't planning on being buried no time soon! So, I ain't wearing it!" End of discussion.

Though all of us tried our best to convince him the suit was beautiful and certainly was not purchased with any thought of using it as a "burying suit," we were wasting our time. As I have pointed out in other writings, of the many personality traits possessed by my dad, being stubborn and headstrong were at the top of the list.

He did not try on the jacket. He did not put on the pants. The suit never came out of the box. It was taken back to the store from which it had been purchased a few days later.

I am happy to report that Dad lived several more years after the "burying suit" was sent back. He did get a new suit some time later but it certainly wasn't Navy blue with white pin-stripes. And, probably because of this one incident, when the time did come that my dad passed away and was laid to rest, he was dressed in one of his favorite blue shirts and jeans. No burying suit was needed.

Our family has enjoyed this memory many times since the "burying suit" was bought and returned. We have often laughed at the thought of how Dad came to think of the suit as a symbol of being ready to meet his maker. And, yes we have shook our heads in amazement at how hard headed that man could be at times. If it is true that we become more like our parents the older we get, then all I can say is God bless all the grand-children of Quincy Lee as their parents get older.

Chapter 40

MOM - THE NURSE IN HER UNDERSTOOD THE BATTLE AHEAD

As mentioned in previous essays, my mother was a registered nurse who had been trained in that profession during the early part of World War II at the Sacred Heart School of Nursing in Pensacola, Florida. Shortly after graduation from nurses' school, she joined the United States Army to serve her country in the war effort. She was stationed in Atlanta, GA where she worked in a hospital providing care for wounded soldiers who had been returned to the states from the battlefields in Europe. Mother was very proud about this service to her country during the war and was very much a patriot for the United States of America during her entire adult life.

After the war ended, she returned to the north Florida area and began her career in public health in Holmes County, Florida where she again served the people around her by providing health care to the citizens of Bonifay and the entire county at a time when the availability of health care in the rural panhandle of Florida was very limited and much needed. She worked in the health department for over 36 years.

After retiring, she enjoyed several years of excellent health. But, as she aged, she began to experience several health issues. In addition to having had high blood pressure for a number of years, she also had an issue with her heart which that was related to her having had rheumatic fever as a child that damaged a valve. This became more troublesome as the years passed. In addition to the heart issue, she also developed arthritis in both of her knees and also had some fairly significant problems with her back.

Ultimately, she ended up having to have one of her knees surgically replaced. Her back continued to deteriorate to the point that if was difficult to walk long distances and it seemed as if back surgery was in the near future. But, little did we know the back was just the tip of the iceberg of her health issues. The heart issues were much more serious than we knew at the time.

During a visit from a home health nurse checking on her back, she left a note for my mom which said something to the effect of "Don't worry about the back but you need to have the heart checked soon." Obviously, this caused my mom (and all of family) to have real concern about what was going on with her heart. She scheduled an appointment with her cardiologist to have it checked.

During the visit with the cardiologist and subsequent follow-up appointments, it was discovered that mom had a serious problem with a heart valve that was not sealing properly. This allowed blood to flow back into the heart after a beat which can lead to blood clots and other serious consequences. In addition, it was discovered that because of the overwork being done by the heart to compensate for the leaking valve, the heart had become very enlarged and had lost the ability to fully compress during a heartbeat. After several visits, it was determined that she needed to have open heart surgery to repair or replace the valve.

Because of the serious nature of the surgery, her cardiologist requested that mom have the required surgery at either the University of Alabama Medical Center in Birmingham or at Emory University in Atlanta, Georgia because these two hospitals had the most highly qualified surgeons in the southeast with the capability to perform the surgery. Mom was reluctant to travel to either of these because of the travel distance that would be required for my dad who was not in good health at the time.

She asked about any other surgeons that were qualified to do the surgery in the north Florida area. Her cardiologist said that the only other hospital that could possibly do the surgery was at the Sacred Heart Hospital if she could get Dr. James Jasper who had been trained at the University of Alabama-Birmingham to do the surgery. We contacted Dr. Jasper and set up an appointment. After seeing mom and looking at her medical records and history, it was decided that mom would have the surgery in Pensacola with Dr. Jasper as the surgeon.

Surgery was scheduled for September 6, 2000 at Sacred Heart Hospital. My sister Janis, my brother Silas, dad and me all were present on the morning of the surgery along with a few other family members. Mom came through the surgery but the news was not good. It was decided that my brother would take dad home and Janis and I stayed in Pensacola overnight to wait on further information from Dr. Jasper. The next morning, we met with him in his office and had a very frank discussion with him about the surgery and the prognosis for recovery. During this visit, he informed us that mom's heart was much more damaged than he believed prior to the surgery. He told us that the echo-cardiogram that had been reviewed by him did not show the extent to which mom's heart was enlarged.

He then told us the damage was so severe that had he known how bad it was prior to the surgery, he would not have performed it. He told us that over half of the people with damage that severe did not survive the operation. He then laid out the prognosis and it was not good. He told us that of the people that survived the surgery, another half of them would die within 6 months to a year. And of those, another 50% would pass away within 2 years. He also said that the damage was so severe that the heart function would be greatly reduced and would lead to a series of congestive heart failure problems that would eventually be too great to overcome and would be the ultimate cause of death for mom. This was a very somber meeting with him and though Janis and I appreciated his honesty, it was difficult to hear.

Of course, with mom being a nurse, it was just a matter of time before she was awake and asking questions about the surgery and her projected recovery time. And, mom was one of those people who did not have much capacity for not knowing the whole story when it came to health issues including her own. After some discussion with Dr. Jasper, it was decided that he would be forthright with her and tell her the truth about her situation.

Upon hearing the news, mom was, as would be expected upset but, fully understanding of what lay ahead. Her background in health care had exposed her many times to people that were facing difficult times ahead. Though she understood the road to be traveled, she did not complain or ever ask "Why me?" about her situation. I know one reason for this ability to have the attitude she did was because of her deep faith in God, knowing that He was in control of everything and whatever happened would be His will.

After a few days, mom was doing some better but it was apparent that she would be in the hospital for some time. Janis and I worked out a schedule where one of us would be there for a few days and then the other one would relieve him or her. In total, mom was in the hospital for about 3 weeks before getting to come home for the first time. Silas did not stay at the hospital with her during this time as he was not comfortable in the role of providing care or in speaking with the hospital staff about the care needs for mom. However, though I knew this then and even better now, this did cause some irritation to develop between him, Janis and me.

In particular, one morning after having been going back and forth for several days, both Janis and I were very tired and just plain worn down. We were both on edge from sheer exhaustion and feeling somewhat put upon because Silas wasn't, or so it seemed at the time, pulling his fair share of the load. As it happened, he showed up that very morning to bring dad to visit mom. When they got to the hospital, dad stayed in the room with mom and the three of us went down to the hospital cafeteria to get something to eat. During the meal, the discussion turned to the time that Janis and I were spending in Pensacola with little to no help from Silas in this. I was trying to be civil and not engage in any hostile words but suddenly, the tiredness, frustration, exhaustion and irritability all came upon me like a ground swell of emotions. And right there in the cafeteria at Sacred Heart Hospital, I proceeded to give me brother a piece of my mind complete with a few choice words and expressions better suited to out behind the barn, not in a public place. Thanks goodness, he had enough sense or understanding to not say anything back to me or we might have thrown down right there. I got up and left to avoid any further confrontation and went back upstairs.

After a little while, my sister came back up to the room and Silas and dad headed back home. When they had left, she started laughing at me and telling me that she had never seen the "little" brother act like that. We both had a good laugh and it probably helped to relieve the tension some for both of us.

But, while we were discussing the incident in the cafeteria, my mom picked up on the conversation and started trying to tell us that she had heard the big commotion that we were talking about. She had been in the hospital for several days by this time and the days and nights were running together for her and she had lost track of time. She was also suffering some from drug induced mental confusion and was not fully engaged cognitively.

Janis and I both tried to tell her that she had not heard the commotion that we were talking about since it had happened in the cafeteria. But, in her state of confusion, she insisted that she had heard it. Janis just passed if off and left the room for a brief time. While she was gone, mom called me up to the head of her bed and then she said something that was quite funny at the time and again provided a moment of levity that was really needed.

She motioned for me to come close to her and then she said to me in a low voice, "I know dang well I heard the commotion that you all are talking about. It happened late last night right outside me room there in the little hallway. It was a big argument that happened between the cowboys and Puerto Ricans." Janis came back in just in time to hear this from mom.

When she said this, both of us just started laughing our heads off. We had to leave the room so as not to upset mom. When we got out of hearing, I made the comment that I had now learned something new about American history. I told Janis that for all of my life I had thought the problem in the early days of the wild west was between the cowboys and Indians. But, mom had just cleared it up for me. The real problem had been between the cowboys and Puerto Ricans.

I must say this was not the only funny thing mom did while in the hospital. She had a very real problem with any medicine that contained a morphine base for pain. It would send her to la-la land or on trips to who knows where. And the funny thing about this was that she would know what it did to her and would know that she would say and do things that did not make rational sense. On one of these occasions, she set straight up in bed and began making motions with her hand as if she was picking something off something else, neither of which was present. When I asked her what she was doing, she replied that she was picking the lights off of her electric purse. Immediately she responded that she knew that did not make any sense at all and just laid her head back down. After a couple of other similar episodes one morning, she told me and Janis to "Tell them doctors to <u>NOT</u> give me any more of that <u>DAMN</u> morphine."

Well, as predicted by Dr. Jasper, mom's health continued to deteriorate over the next few months. She would have an episode of congestive heart failure, end up in the hospital for a few days to remove the fluid from her lungs and chest cavity, take some medication, get better and go home. Then, she would begin to show signs of congestion again, go to the hospital, get some better and return home. This happened several times between September and December with the cycle repeating itself and her getting a little weaker with each succeeding episode.

And, again because of her background in healthcare, she was fully aware of what was happening. She began to talk with us about the time that she would not be able to recover and was insistent that we not put her through the ordeal of doing anything in the way of putting her on life support or performing any heroic treatment to simply prolong her life for a few days.

On December 6, 2000, another round of congestive heart failure began. It was obvious that this was more serious than previous times and within a short time it was evident that this would likely end in her death. She did not go to Pensacola for this last round in the hospital but instead insisted to only go to the hospital in Bonifay. Janis, Silas and I stayed with her around the clock with other family members coming in from time to time. Dad could not stand to see her in the condition she was in and would visit only briefly and go home. Her breathing was labored and very difficult to watch.

As the end neared, she could be heard faintly repeating the 23rd Psalm. She passed from this world to eternity on December 8, 2000.

This was the worst day of my life up until that point in time. I had just lost my mom and the realization that I would never be able to see her again or eat one of her meals or just talk to her broke my heart beyond my ability to describe. I had lost the person who had literally been with me from my first breath on this earth never to be with her again until I joined her in heaven.

But, in the days following, I was comforted by the fact that my mom always loved me and was a great mom. She always wanted the best for me and would do anything in her power to help me in any way possible. I was blessed to have her as a parent.

I thank God daily for letting me have Gertrude M. Lee as my mom.

Chapter 41

⌘

GERTRUDE M. LEE EULOGY
AND NEWSPAPER ARTICLES

Gertrude M. Lee

Eulogy

December 8, 2000

On behalf of my Dad, Janis, Silas, I, our wives and husbands, the grandchildren and our entire extended family, thanks more than words can ever express for all of your love, prayers, calls and visits during this very difficult time for us. This support and love has made it possible for us to carry on, even though it seemed, at times, that we could go no further.

While this has been a very difficult and sad time, it has also been a time of reflection on the life of our Mother. And it has been a celebration, of sorts, for the life of one of God's true servants. Jesus told his disciples in Matthew 20:26 that whoever wanted to be great among them, must be their servant. And in Ephesians 6:7-8, Paul writes, "Serve wholeheartedly, as if you were serving the Lord, not men, because you know that the Lord will reward everyone for whatever good he does." If ever there was a person with a servant heart for her family, community and country, it was my mom.

This servant hood was shown in many ways throughout her life. Early on, after being the first in her family to graduate from high school at Vernon in 1941, she went to nursing school, paying her own way, so that she could begin to serve others as a health care professional. Shortly after finishing nursing school, she joined the U. S. Army as an army nurse at the end of World War II and served her country and fellow citizens as a member of the armed services. And believe me, she was proud that she had been able to serve her country in this way.

After finishing her tour of duty in the military as a 2nd Lieutenant, she came to Holmes County to begin another career of service as a county health nurse. She continued in this job for 36+ years, beginning on April 1, 1946 and retiring on June 24, 1982 as the Director of Holmes County Health Department. But, when she began this job, it was not quite the same as it is today. In fact, when she began this job, there were only 2 or 3 paved roads in Holmes County. And her job, along with Mrs. Norma Sims and Mrs. Ruby Bedford, was to take health care out to the people in the county. And take health care out to the people, they did. They went to the schools, stores, community centers, churches, countless homes and anywhere else needed to make sure that people in the rural part of North Florida began to receive health care. To put it another way, my mom was home health care before there was such a thing as home health care.

The impact their efforts had on the health of the citizens of Holmes County was tremendous. From treating illnesses, making referrals to doctors, sending doctors to see people who were found to be sick and bringing people back to town with them in their cars to see the doctor. And who can tell the impact of one of their most important missions — the immunizations for children of childhood diseases. Everyone in the schools in Holmes County in the late 40's, 50's, 60's, 70's and maybe even into the 80's knew who Mrs. Lee was. They may not have known her name, but they knew she was that lady who always gave us the shots. Though it may have been a little pain for them at the time, there is no doubt that it saved some of their lives and improved the quality of life for most of them.

I just have to share one story with you that mom loved to tell. Early on in this job, she had to go up the river road over in Westville up to Cerra Gorda, the Cullifer community and New Hope. This was a dirt road back then and travel was difficult. As she was driving along, she began to hear guns or some other types of small explosions taking place. This happened all along the road. Well, this happened a couple of times on trips over there. Finally, one day while stopped at the store in the Cullifer community, she asked Mrs. Cullifer about these sounds. Mrs. Cullifer said, "Aw, Mrs. Lee that is just the boys warning the others that there is a strange car in the neighborhood. They didn't know if you was a "revenuer" or not. Don't worry. You want hear them no more." And, that was the last time she heard it. The people over there knew that she was someone they could trust and she was there to help.

In this job, she also did many things beyond the call of duty to serve her community. I remember many nights of her talking on the phone to Dr. Simpson, Dr. Groover, Dr. Nelson, Mrs. Sims and others, trying to get help for some family or child who needed it. I remember many times when she took children and their parents on her car to what was then known as the "Crippled Children's Clinic" over in Pensacola for treatment. She was a "doer of the word" in that she didn't just talk about getting things done to help people. She saw that they were done and wasn't real good at taking no for an answer. Many of the people she helped, especially those who were taken to the crippled children's clinic will tell you that if it hadn't been for mom, they would never have made it. There are too many of these cases to even begin to tell about individual cases, but the bottom line of this is that my mom took care of people.

Though I would not have enough time to begin to outline all of the services she helped bring to Holmes County, I do want to share two with you. She was the force behind and served as the director of the first study of high blood pressure – hypertension diseases in Holmes, Washington and Walton counties in the late 1960's. This one effort, carried out by the health departments of those counties, was responsible for screening and identifying 1000's of people in our area who were referred on for treatment of high blood pressure and heart disease. There is no way to describe the positive impact that this effort had in these 3 counties, literally saving the lives of many. This study was so highly regarded that it received publication in the American Journal of Nursing, a national health and medical care magazine.

Also, she, along with several others in our community, were the people who built the Mariner Health Care Center (nursing home) in Bonifay. This facility continues to provide health care for many citizens of our area on a daily basis. She was a member of many professional organizations including the Holmes County Development Commission, the Bonifay Woman's Club, the Big Bend Health Council, Florida Health Council, the Florida Nurses Association, the American Nurses Association and too many others to name. She was recognized in 1975 as the Community Health Worker of the Year for the entire state of Florida. And, in 1997 she was asked to speak at a statewide meeting at the University of South Florida and give a report on the history of public health care in the state of Florida.

Gertrude Lee was a recognized leader in community health all over this state. And, she was trusted at home by her peers. When there was a need for a new health department building in Holmes County, my mom asked to present this need to the county commission at a meeting. After she had finished her presentation, Commissioner John Clark said something to the effect of, "If Mrs. Lee said we need a new health department, then we must need one. I make a motion to build a new health department." The motion was seconded and passed 5-0. There was no money for a new health department in the budget, no plans at that time, no impact study, no nothing. Just the word from a trusted source that it was needed. And, it was built. And, it was named the "**<u>Gertrude M. Lee Health Center</u>**". What an honor!

But, this was not the only area of servant hood for mom. She was also a servant and leader in our community, better known as the County Line Community or the Bethel Church Community.

Now uptown, mom was a nurse. But, believe me, in our community, she was "Doctor Lee". And, she had several specialties. She was a pediatrician, did a little internal medicine, some psychiatry and counseling, a little bit of veterinary medicine, orthopedics and many minor surgeries. These "surgeries" were mostly of the removing foreign objects from various parts of the body variety. She made house calls free of charge, made many referrals to other doctors, dispensed medicine, treated the flu, viruses, fever and all other types of illnesses. And as we were talking the other night as a family, she never shied away from any ailment. If someone called, she went.

I have to share this favorite family tale with you. Some of you have heard it before, but it is worth hearing again. My dad had been working outside and had stuck a large splinter under his fingernail, all the way up past the base of the nail on his middle finger. It was some kind of hurting. Well, they got the splinter out, but over the next few days, it began to hurt and developed an infection. My dad had this brilliant idea of how to cure this infection.

Now this next part is not for the faint of heart. He went to my mom and said, "Woman, I want you to take a syringe and hypodermic needle, fill it with methylate, slide it up under my nail, right where that splinter was and fill it up." My mom said, "Quincy, I am not going to do that. It will hurt so bad you won't be able to stand it." He said, "Well, it is hurting so bad now I can't stand it, so just do what I said." You know dad. Not a stubborn bone in his body and just do it his way and quit arguing.

"Well, okay, if that's what you really want, but I'm telling you, you won't be able to stand it." said mom. So she filled the needle full and did just what he wanted. Well, when the methylate hit the finger, it was just as bad as mom thought and a lot worse than my dad thought. He began to sling his hand, dance around and he said ….

Well, he said he thought the methylate would work — or something to that effect. For exactly what he said, you will have to ask some of us outside of the church. I don't believe I ought to use those words in here. Needless to say, my mom had the laugh of a lifetime about this little surgery and shared it with many.

She was also a leader in her church and our community. She was active in this church for many years, serving in many capacities. And through her and many of you, this church was the foundation of our family's faith and the source that began our individual faith journeys.

She was a good neighbor and tried her best to help those around her.

She cooked for the cattleman's association annual director's meeting that was held at our house for many years. This was always around Christmas time and it was always a big gathering of friends. Mr. Ferrell Nelson said there was no telling how many pick-up truckloads of biscuits she had made for these famous suppers. And after the meal, they would all gather around the piano and sing Christmas carols. Memories of great times, with good friends.

I want to say just one more word about this community in which we had the privilege to be raised. All of our family wishes to say to all of you with all of our hearts how much we love you. Our foundations of life are right here in the Bethel Church / County Line Road community and have been for several generations. The things we believe, those values that we hold dear, such as love, support for one another, honesty, integrity, being good neighbors, and too many others to name, and those very deep beliefs that we hold on to tightly when the storms of life buffet us about, are as a result of being raised in this community with this group of people. If ever there was a community that believed, by word and deed, that it takes the whole community to raise children, this it that community.   And I can tell you that when I need to go "home" for safety or support, it is always in my heart and mind to go home to this community of family and friends.

But, it was her servant hood to her family that is the most special to us.   She was a great teacher about life. She was a great seamstress, a great mother and wife, an artist and the best cook that has ever been. If they eat in heaven, today someone is eating the best creamed corn ever, some great turkey and dressing, excellent seafood gumbo, a super peanut butter cake - and maybe the occasional piece of burned toast for breakfast. Maybe that old oven in heaven won't get so hot so quick.

My mom believed in family. She was always concerned about the welfare of her whole family, including husband, children, grandchildren, sisters, brothers, nieces and nephews and all the others. In fact, she gave us all some instructions to follow on Thursday while she was in the hospital.   And the sum total of what she said to us was just what Jesus told us in his word. "Love one another."

My mom also believed in the Lord with all her heart. One of her favorite verses in the Bible was Romans 8:28 which says, "And we know that in all things God works for the good of those who love him, who have been called according to his purpose." And she would often follow this with, "And I trust you are called to His purpose." And we trust that this valley we are going through was also according to His purpose.

In closing, on Friday, the Lord, with open arms, told my mom, "Welcome home, my good and faithful servant." She is home and resting today. And, though sad beyond words, there is joy that we will see her again.

Thank you for being here to honor her life. Thank you for your love, support and friendship through the years. Please keep us all in your prayers.

Gertrude M. Lee
Obituary
Newspaper Article

Mrs. Gertrude M. Lee, a long time community leader in Holmes County, passed away after a lengthy illness on December 8, 2000 at Doctor's Memorial Hospital. Mrs. Lee is survived by her husband of 53 years, Mr. James Quincy Lee, son-in-law and daughter Wayne and Janis Johnson, son and wife Silas and Kim Lee, son and wife Bill and Frances M. Lee, 8 grand children and 1 great grand child.

Mrs. Lee began her career of service in Holmes County on April 1, 1946 as a nurse at the Holmes County Health Department. She came to Holmes County after serving her country as a nurse during World War II as a member of the United States Army, finishing her military duty as a 2nd Lieutenant. Along with Mrs. Norma Sims and Mrs. Ruby Bedford, she was a pioneer in the field of public health for Holmes County. Mrs. Lee continued in this service for 36+ years, retiring in June 1982 as the director of the Holmes County Health Department.

During her tenure at the Holmes County Health Department, Mrs. Lee was instrumental in bringing many improvements in health care to the citizens of Holmes County. She was a leader in having the children in our county receiving immunizations for communicable diseases such as diphtheria, small pox and measles. She was also instrumental in helping to put an end to the most dreaded disease at that time for children - polio. Mrs. Lee worked to put an end to other illnesses which affected the everyday lives of people such as hook worms, pin worms and other diseases which were caused by unhealthy living conditions.

Mrs. Lee made countless visits to homes, county schools, community centers and churches during her career in public health to help the citizens of our county to have healthier lives. In fact, most of the children who attended school in Holmes County in the late 1940's, 1950's, 1960's and 1970's knew who Mrs. Lee was. They may not have known her name, but they all knew she was "that lady who gave us the shots". The impact that these shots had on the lives of the boys and girls of this county is hard to measure. It was a few moments of pain for them that allowed all of them to have a better quality of life.

Mrs. Lee was also a recognized leader in public health for the entire state of Florida. She was the person who headed up the first effort in Holmes, Walton and Washington counties to identify and get treatment for people with high blood pressure and hypertension. This program, which began in 1969, identified hundreds or maybe even thousands of people in these three counties of rural north Florida who had heart disease or high blood pressure and needed treatment. If not for Mrs. Lee, many of these people would never have known of their illnesses or received treatment. This one effort alone saved countless lives and was recognized nationally by publication in the American Journal of Nursing.

Mrs. Lee was a member of many local and state organizations. She was a long time member and past president of the Bonifay Woman's Club. She served on the Holmes County Development Commission and was a member of the Holmes County Cancer Society. She was also a member of the North Florida Health Council, the Big Bend Health Council, the Florida Nurses Association and the American Nurses Association. Even after retirement, she was active in other health organizations such as the Epilepsy Foundation.

In 1975, Mrs. Lee was selected by her peers of the Florida Nurses Association as the Public Health Care Nurse of the Year for the state of Florida. And, in 1997, she received a special invitation from the University of South Florida in Tampa to be the presenter on the history of public health care in the state of Florida.

Mrs. Lee was also committed to getting service for many people in Holmes County who did not know where to go. Many citizens were assisted by her when they needed help getting to doctors or clinics for treatment. Mrs. Lee even took many of these on her personal automobile for treatment, including numerous trips with children and their families to the "Crippled Children's Clinic" in Pensacola, Florida for assistance with serious health problems.

The health services that Mrs. Gertrude Lee brought to the citizens of Holmes County are too numerous to list them all. But two that continue to help the people of our county on a daily basis are the health department building in Bonifay and the Mariner Health Care Center or nursing home. Mrs. Lee was the driving force behind the construction of the new health department building in the early 1980's. This effort brought new and improved services for health care to the citizens of Holmes County and continues to be a source of health care today. In fact, Mrs. Lee was honored by the county for her efforts in this by having the building named after her. It is now known as the "Gertrude M. Lee Health Center.

She was also a member of a small group of citizens who obtained funding to construct the nursing home in Bonifay and this facility continues to provide for the needs of many people and their families.

Funeral services were held on Monday, December 11, 2000 at Bethel Primitive Baptist Church where Mrs. Lee was an active, long time member with Rev. Jesse Stanaland and Rev. Larry Anderson presiding. The eulogy was given by her son, Bill Lee. Active pallbearers were Eric McCullough, Emory McCullough, Tony McCullough, John Bush, Buddy McCullough, Sammy Lee, Tommy Beasley and Harrell Hammond. Honorary pallbearers were former and present employees of the Holmes County Health Department who worked with Mrs. Lee and members of the Holmes-Washington Cattlemen's Association.

Gertrude McCullough Lee
A Nurse for the People of Holmes County

Gertrude McCullough was born on November 13, 1922 in rural Washington County, Florida near Vernon, the 7th of 11 children born to Felton and Roxie Smothers McCullough. Gertrude attended school in Vernon and was the first person in her family to graduate from high school in 1941. After graduation, she worked and saved money to attend nursing school, graduating from Sacred Heart in Pensacola, Florida. She enlisted in the U.S. Army as a 2nd Lieutenant and served as an Army nurse during World War II in Atlanta, Georgia, treating soldiers returning from overseas. After her Army service, she returned home and accepted a job with the Holmes County Health Department on April 1, 1946.

She also met and married her husband, James Quincy Lee in March, 1947. They lived their lives together for 53 years on the family farm that had been homesteaded by Quincy's parents, Silas and Della Lee. They had three children, Janis Dianne, Silas Dill and James Willie (Bill) Lee.

Gertrude M. Lee made a lasting mark on the history of Holmes County in her capacity as a nurse with the health department. When she accepted the job, there were few paved roads in the county, travel was difficult, and few health care services were provided to the outlying areas. Except for extreme emergencies, people did not make visits to town to see a doctor and the same was true for medical personnel going to the people's homes.

Gertrude Lee, Norma Sims, Rupert Padgett and Ruby Moore were the people who worked at the health department, beginning in the late 1940's, that began to change the health outlook for the rural citizens. These four people began to travel throughout the county providing much needed medical services, including primary care for minor injuries, diseases such as measles and mumps, infections and fever. Mr. Padgett helped to improve health throughout the county in his work as the county health inspector.

Gertrude, Norma and Ruby made regular trips to all of the county schools, making sure that school children were up to date on their immunizations, doing screenings for referrals to other medical providers and providing training to school personnel on health related issues. Many children in these schools came to know the types of cars that Mrs. Lee and Mrs. Sims drove and knew when they saw those cars, someone was going to get a shot. Mrs. Lee once reported that she had probably seen more rear ends of kids in Holmes County than most people had seen faces.

Gertrude would often see children who were in severe need of extensive medical treatment. These medical problems were often the result of polio, congenital birth defects, poor hygiene in the home environment or the result of severe infections. In response to these observed needs, she would put into action her belief that she was called to help improve the quality of life of the people she served. She would make referrals to area hospitals and doctors to get these children treated for their conditions. She would take children on her own car to Pensacola to the Crippled Children's Clinic or would arrange for doctors to make the necessary home visits. She went beyond the call of duty for these children to insure that their health care needs were met.

Many of the people that were the beneficiaries of these services would make contact with Gertrude after they had become adults to personally thank her for her help while they were children. She often spoke of helping people who had gone on to great successes in their adult lives after severe medical challenges early in life and was proud that she had been a small part of these successes.

Gertrude Lee was also instrumental in helping to improve the health of all citizens of Holmes County. She was one of the first people in our area to begin the process of hook worm eradication by working with other area leaders to help get livestock laws passed so that animals were penned up rather than being allowed to roam freely. This program also involved educating families on the importance of personal hygiene and the advantages of indoor plumbing and septic tanks.

Mrs. Lee was also a leader in public health for the entire state of Florida. She headed up the first effort in Holmes, Walton and Washington counties to identify and get treatment for people with high blood pressure and hypertension. This program, which began in 1969, was started because of her concern for the number of individuals in our area that were dying as a result of stroke and heart attack. The study was conducted over a period of many months by going to all areas of the county and doing free blood pressure checks at area schools, country stores, churches and community gatherings. It identified hundreds or maybe thousands of people in these three counties who had heart disease or high blood pressure and needed treatment. Many of these people would never have known of their illnesses or received treatment. This one effort alone saved countless lives and was recognized nationally by publication in the American Journal of Nursing.

In 1975, Mrs. Lee was selected by her peers as the Public Health Care Nurse of the Year for the state of Florida. This is the highest award presented by the Florida Nurses Association. In 1997, she received a special invitation from the University of South Florida in Tampa to be the presenter on the history of public health care in the state of Florida.

Gertrude Lee retired in June 1982 after 36 years of dedicated service with the Holmes County Health Department, where she had served as the Director of Nursing for a number of years. Shortly before her retirement, she had started the process of obtaining funding for the construction of a new health department building to replace a facility that was no longer adequate to meet the health care needs of the citizens of Holmes County. The building was completed in 1984 and was named the Gertrude M. Lee Health Center in her honor.

Gertrude Lee passed away on December 8, 2000. She left behind a legacy of love and service for her county and her family. She was a true pioneer in health care for the citizens of Holmes County and surrounding areas.

Chapter 42

CHANGING RELATIONSHIPS IN FAMILIES

I have been considering a life reality for the last few months about the relationships between parents and their children. As ones parents age, they move toward dependence on their children. The relationship changes that take place because of this are among the most difficult challenges in life for both the parent and child or children. These relationship changes are difficult at best, impossible at worst and filled with emotional stress for all involved.

The reasons that this has been on my mind lately has been the continuing deterioration of my father's health the last few months. It seems that more and more of my sister's, brother and my time lately has been spent as a taxi, taking my dad back and forth to some doctor's appointment or hospital stay. This changing relationship between the parent and children has been the focal point of many of these visits. This is because my dad, never a real good patient even when younger, has become increasingly resistant to doctor visits, even when it has been demonstrated to him that it is a necessity.

This change from provider, guardian, protector, family head, and all other similar roles filled by parents to one in which the child fills these roles for the elderly parent is a process that requires great love, patience, persistence, compassion, and tolerance. Particularly on the part of the children, though this is probably true on the part of the parents also, though I have not had the opportunity to be in that role. Yet! Ask me again in about another 30 years if I am so blessed to make it that long here on the earth. It also requires more than a little bit of understanding and humor, for these two may hold the keys to being able to survive these trying and difficult times.

From the perspective of the parent, it has to be very frustrating to have to depend upon the children that they brought into the world to take care of them. This is not the normal human understanding of how the parent and child relationship works. Also, many of these elderly people hate to feel that they are becoming a burden to those around them. It can also be humiliating to the elderly parent, having to have their own children attending to their most personal needs such as bathing them and meeting other sanitary needs.

As is the case with my dad, most people of this present generation of elderly people, grew up in a time when it was a fact of life that you had to do for yourself. They were raised in the era of the great depression and shortly after that period of time was World War II, the greatest conflict that the world has ever known. It was during the times following these two events that helped to shape the lives of this generation that they began to raise families of their own. The people who grew up during these times were, by nature and necessity, an independent, strong willed, hard-headed, self-providing group. Now that they have reached the age where they often have to depend on others to do for them, it is very difficult for them to change.

When my dad returned home after the war, he came back to the same farm from which he had left with the family still there, pretty much how he had left it, including both his dad and mom and his brother, Homer Lee, who was some 11 years older than dad. Uncle Homer had been living and working on this farm with my Pa and Ma his entire life and when my dad returned, Uncle Homer was approximately 37 years. But even though he (Uncle Homer) was much older than dad and had been working on the farm his entire life, it was not long before my dad assumed the leadership role for the family and in the process became the defacto "boss" of the Lee clan. I heard the story many times of how this change in leadership of the family farm took place and the long and short of the reason is this – my dad was an "alpha male", natural leader who was not very good at taking directions from other people. He wanted to be in charge, was stubborn to a fault, and was a person that was very comfortable in being the boss. My Uncle Homer was much more of a follower and doer than a leader and recognized, I suppose, that dad was going to be the boss one way or the other.

So, with this background of information, one may more readily see that the changing in the relationships between my dad and us because of him growing older and his failing health was not an easy road for him to travel. He was used to being in charge of all aspects of his life for the last 70 years and was not about to let go of this easily.

The culmination of this for him and us was the fact that he had a stroke in the fall of 2008 that left him partially immobile though he was not paralyzed. The stroke weakened him to the point that he was no longer able to walk unassisted at all even though he could stand up and sit down in a chair, move himself to a bed in a wheelchair, and get out of the chair into either his bed or a recliner without assistance. He could feed himself without assistance but did have to have assistance with bodily sanitary functions (bathing and using the restroom).

As a result of this stroke, he was in the hospital for a number of days, then transferred to a rehabilitation unit for a few weeks and was then sent back to a hospital "swing" bed unit for a few more days to try and build up his strength to hopefully be able to go back home where he had been living independently prior to the stroke and for several years following the death of mom in December 2000.

But, after several more days in rehab, it became apparent that he was not going to be able to go back home to live independently anymore and in fact, would have to be placed in a facility that provided skilled nursing and care. While in the swing bed unit, because of Medicare or Medicaid rules, dad had almost reached the time limit for which he could remain in the hospital. Just a day or two before he had reached the time limit, a private room became available at the nursing home in Bonifay and my sister and I made the decision that we would take the room and tell dad that he would be transferred to the facility the next day. Even though this was really our only option, other than to have him moved to another nursing home in Graceville, Chipley, or some other town further from home, we knew that he was going to be very upset about this news as he had always told us that he never, ever wanted to be placed in a nursing home.

So, we called the nursing home and told them we wanted the room and went to inform dad of this decision. As we expected, dad was very upset with this news, was very angry with us, said he was not going to go, and blamed us for not taking him home where he wanted to go. We tried every way possible to explain the reasons for the decision to have him transferred to the nursing home but we might as well have engaged him in a conversation about nuclear physics and how to build an atomic bomb. He was not interested in listening to us and had his mind made up – he wanted to go home and blamed Janis and me for not taking him there.

Dad was transferred to the Bonifay Nursing Home the next day and remained as a patient there for almost 2 full years. I could go into a lot of details about this time but just suffice it to say that he hated every second of every minute of every day of every week that he stayed in the nursing home. And, though he reportedly told other people he knew that he needed to be there, he never told me or Janis this and often would tell us that "You all put me here." Though we explained many, many times that he could not go home because of his health, he never accepted this as fact. We offered to let him come live with us, we offered let him live with one of us a while and then the other one a while, we always got the same an-swer – "I want to go home."

To say that these almost two years were some of the most difficult ones that I had ever lived would not be an exaggeration. It was difficult on him and us. Even when in the nursing home, we would sometimes have to take him to the doctor or other medical appointments. Each and every time we had to do this, we would be asked to take him home and just let him stay there. In his mind, someone could just come by and check on him and he would be okay even though he had to have someone assist him with virtually every daily living activity.

The changing of roles in this ongoing life challenge was difficult on all involved. It was hardest on dad but was also hard on my sister, brother and me. We did not necessarily want to be the ones with the decision making responsibility for dad, but it was something we had to do. He really did not want us making the decisions we made about and for him, but it was just what had to be done at the time. It is ironic, that during this time, Janis, Silas, and I could all recall very vividly when my dad and mom made these same types of decisions for both my paternal and mater-nal grandparents in the latter years of their lives. Life truly does move in cycles I guess.

Well, in a few years, if I am blessed to live out a somewhat normal life expectancy, I will likely be the one who is taking orders from my children or grandchildren in regards to my health or business affairs. Just like my dad, I probably will not be very good at it though I would hope that I am not quite as vocal about it as he was.

Chapter 43

JAMES QUINCY LEE EULOGY

James Quincy Lee
July 7, 1920 – February 3, 2008

On behalf of Janis, Silas, our wives and husbands, the grandchildren, great-grandchildren and our entire extended family, thanks more than words can ever express for all of your love, prayers, calls and visits during this very difficult time for us. I am proud to be able to do this eulogy for my dad on behalf of our family. I trust that the next few minutes will be a time of celebration for the life of dad and that it will cause all of you to reflect on your own personal memories of him.

James Quincy Lee, Daddy, Big Pa, J.Q., Uncle Quincy, Quinc. This was a man who was large in stature and lived life in a large way. He was strong as a bull in his younger years before the ravages of age took its toll with arms the size of most people's legs, legs like tree trunks, and hands like bear claws. He was direct as you can get, talented in so many ways, a prankster who loved to laugh and enjoyed life, had the pain threshold of an elephant, and was a friend to many. He was a veteran of the US Navy, having proudly served in WWII in the south Pacific. He was a die-hard Democrat who liked some Republicans but voted for none of them. He would have been happy for all men to be bald headed and all people to be Democrats. And though, what you saw was what you got, he was also a man of contrasts, a complex man who was much more than what you may have seen on the surface.

To his family, he was husband, dad, Big Pa, and uncle. Coming out of the Navy after WWII, he returned to the family farm where he just sort of took over even though he was the baby of the family, being some eight years younger than Uncle John D, the next youngest child and who is now 95. I guess this was because of his lifelong way of doing things his way. Uncle Homer, Ma, Pa and all the others who were around at that time probably knew it was a waste of their time and effort to try to do it another way. Because, as all of you that knew dad know, there were two ways to do things around daddy, his way and his way. But, in retrospect, this stubborn refusal to compromise, especially on the important things of life, made it possible for our family to move forward and to become successful. He was the glue that held his large extended family together.

He married Mom shortly after coming back home from the Navy and the two of them were like grits and eggs, peanut butter and jelly, and salt and pepper. They complimented each other because of their differences. Momma was one of the few people who could put Daddy in his place just by the way she would say, "Now, Quincy!" when she had had enough. Their marriage of 53 + years set an example for us to follow on commitment, love, and caring through the good times and the bad.

He was talented in so many ways it is hard to believe. He could build just about anything he wanted to out of metal having learned this trade in the Navy. He could cook just about anything, especially meats, BBQ, steaks, stews, turnip greens, and such. He could can fruits and vegetables, make homemade wine, and put up stuff for the freezer. He could butcher anything with four legs and a hide. When he killed hogs, he would use everything but the squeal and the hair. Hog head cheese, liver and lights, brains and eggs, cracklings, and his personal favorite, chittlins. My how he loved them with pepper sauce! As a matter of fact, he would lots rather have had those things than the ham or the pork chops. My sister Janis lovingly referred to all of these as the "trash" of the hog which would irritate him to no end. Of course, I can't leave this subject without mentioning that he was the best sausage maker in the world, hands down, no offense to some of you who may be here today that think you can make sausage.

Same thing with beef, he used everything but the moo. He loved hash, tripe, liver, and stew beef. He also absolutely loved a big ol' steak, rare as you can get it with some Worcestershire sauce, a potato and a salad. He was an outdoorsman who loved to fish and hunt, especially with James Boswell, who was his best lifelong friend. He loved to hunt quail and shoot dove and he took me and Silas with him many times while we were growing up. He bought each of us a Browning shotgun when we were old enough to hunt with him and taught us how to use them in a safe manner. This love of his for the outdoors has been passed right on down through the years to many of us, especially his grandson Brad.

Dad loved to laugh and was a prankster all the time. He enjoyed a good practical joke either done by him or pulled on him. If you were outside working, he would spray you with a water hose in a New York minute whether it was summer or winter, hot or cold, early or late. And if you were able to do the same to him, he would enjoy the laugher either way. However, he would always say, "All right, just remember, you will pay for that!" I remember one time when I snuck into the bathroom and poured a whole glass of ice cold water over the top while he was showering. It just took his breath. When he came out, he was just laughing out loud and said, "You know you will pay for that." I did a few days later with a return dousing of ice, cold water in the shower.

He loved his grandchildren and kids in general. I remember when Chris and Brad were born and beginning to grow up, we used to say what happened to the people that used to live here when we were children? He would just let them do anything they wanted to do and provide the means for them to do it. With all of the grandchildren, he would tease them, play with them, and generally aggravate them. He would draw pictures of pigs, rabbits, and turkeys on their bellies or faces with a felt tip marker. He would give the girls a dollar for a kiss on the cheeks.

Tell about Abby standing him down for her dollar before the kiss. One of the few times I ever saw anyone more stubborn than him. This should have given me a warning that I was going to get to live with someone just like Quincy Lee again.

If he loved you, it was likely that he gave you a nick name of some kind, some of these that I can't say in church. Whistlebritches, Knothead, Tusshog, Shortstop, Blondie, Rose, Lilly and Pink. He referred to Wayne as "his orphaned son-in-law" after my mom died. He used to hang Tommy Bush up on the picket fence by his belt loops and make him cry to get off one time or not cry to get off the next time. He would get you to pull his finger and be ready to finish the job, complete with sounds and smells to follow.

He had a colorful vocabulary that some would consider profane but with him, it was not intended in that way. He just expressed himself in some pretty direct ways. When he would use a four letter word, most of the time it was so that you could really just understand what he meant in a clear and concise manner. When they were little boys, he loved nothing more than to get Brad and Chris to say a curse word in the presence of Janis so that she would fuss at him for teaching them to curse. He would just belly laugh at this. He would also speak pretty straight to Silas and me once in a while when we were growing up, especially if we had left some of his tools lying around after we had used them to work on our old bicycle or some other project. He would also speak straight up to any other children who happened to be around the home place when they did something that he perceived as in need of attention including the grandchildren.

Many times while I was a principal, I encountered people who would come to my office and say something like, "I can't do a thing with my child. He won't pay any attention to me and he won't mind." At those times, I often wanted to say, "Well, that boy should have been raised at Route 1, Bonifay, Florida by Quincy Lee because it never crossed his mind that he couldn't do something with Janis, Silas, or me."

Dad also had the pain tolerance of an elephant. He got all of his dental work done with no painkiller of any kind including root canals and having his teeth pulled for dentures. He would smash his finger with a hammer, say a few choice words, and keep on working. However, I do remember one of the favorite stories of his pain endurance that my mom loved to tell.

Splinter up the finger nail story.

But this bear of a man had a heart as tender as a momma's love. He hated to see people be mistreated and if you ever mistreated him or his family, he would write you off. He was generous to a fault and would give the shirt off his back to help someone in need. Last night, I don't know how many people came by and related stories of how dad had helped them in a time of need. I know that many of you here today can think back to times that my dad stepped up to help you, too.

It is said that a man is lucky if he can count his friends on one hand at the end of his life. Well, my dad would have had to have had a lot of hands based on the expressions shared with our family last night and as evidenced by the crowd here today.

And though he was not a man to talk very much about religion, he was possibly the best person that I knew at living an example of serving his fellow man. He loved southern gospel music, especially the Cathedrals and George Younce and the Bill Gaither series. He enjoyed going up to Thomasville, GA, sitting on the front row, and hearing the songs. This big bear of a man would tear up and cry as the music played.

His view of the world was mostly black and white with very little grey. You were either what you professed to be or you weren't. He respected people for what they were, not for what they said they were. He believed strongly that a man was only as good as his word. To put this in another way, he did not suffer fools lightly. He tried his best to treat people right and had little patience for those people who professed to be one thing but lived their life in another way.

But, this hard headed, stubborn, obstinate, and unreasonable man was the foundation that held our entire family together. His word was law and his uncompromising standard of life taught us children how to treat our fellow man. His examples of respect for his own mom and dad helped us to understand the importance of family that we all still carry with us today. The stakes of life that he helped all of us to drive down deep into the soil of the Lee Family Farm have been the anchors to which we have tied our ropes as we have faced our own storms of life. We are going to miss him so much.

As he was getting ready to go into surgery, we had a few moments to spend with him and typical of daddy, he had the last word. We each were telling him we loved him, would see him when he came out, and then, Janis said a prayer with all of us around him. When she finished, he looked up at us and, with typical directness, he said, 'Now, Haul _____!" meaning for us to go ahead and leave him alone. So with that, I will tell you the same thing that he would say to encourage you to keep on keeping on, even when the times are tough, to keep the memories of dad alive for the good times you may have shared with him, and to hold on to the pretty high moral standards that he set for all who knew him. Haul _____!

ORDER OF SERVICE

Opening Prayer – Dr. Jeff Spicer

Congregational Song – This World Is Not My Home

Scripture Reading – Dr. Jeff Spicer

Song – Amazing Grace – Abby Lee, Anna Lee, Meredith Lee

Service Message – Jeep Sullivan

Song – Going Home CD

Eulogy – Bill Lee

Closing Prayer – Jeep Sullivan

Graveside Services – Dr. Jeff Spicer

Chapter 44

ONE YEAR AGO TODAY I LOST MY DAD

Today, February 3, 2009, has been a day of remembrances for me as it was one year ago today that my dad passed away. It doesn't seem that it has been a year already since his passing as I still catch myself wanting to call him or go see him as if he were still alive. It has been an extremely quick year in many respects and one of great turmoil in others.

As I consider the last year, I still have trouble putting into words how the death of my father has affected me in the deepest part of my being. He was the last of my parents to pass away with my mother having died in December, 2000. There is still a feeling in my heart of loneliness with both of my parents gone. How I wish I could see them, talk to them, laugh with them, share with them, hug my mom, and ask them for advice one more time.

About a year and a half before my dad passed away, he had suffered a slight stroke. Though this stroke did not paralyze him, it did weaken him to the point of having to have full-time medical care for the remainder of his life.

This need for medical care caused him to be placed in a nursing home for the last several months of his life. He absolutely hated every minute of time he had to spend in the nursing home. This hatred for being in the treatment facility manifested itself into resentment and this resentment of being placed in the nursing home was directed largely at my sister and me as we were the ones who made the decision for placement. Though this placement was an absolute necessity because of his medical needs, my dad never accepted this fact. He believed that he could not return to his house and be allowed to live as he wished with a little care provided by visiting medical personnel from time to time.

Since Janis and I were the people that he pointed the finger at for being placed in a nursing home, he often would express his feelings to us about the unfairness of what we were doing to him. He even told us on several occasions that he had fought during World War II for the freedoms of our great country and now he was being treated as a person with no rights at all.

I have heard many people over the years explain that middle age is when a person is caught in between their own children and their parents. By far, the toughest part of this is trying to be the parent of your parent, especially if the parents are anything like my dad was. To say the least, he was not a very good patient during this time in his life.

Though he would often tell others that he knew he needed to be in the nursing home and would tell visitors that he was not able to go home, he never, not one time, said this to Janis or me. I guess it was just his way of holding on to that last bit of independence from his children telling him what to do and when to do it.

Leading up to the time of dad's sickness that ultimately was the reason for his death, he had been doing pretty good. There was no real indication that he had a serious problem brewing. In fact, Janis and I had some discussions that he might even be in the nursing home for a lengthy period of time and were concerned about this because of his dislike (*yeah, dislike*) for the facility.

As it turned out, he developed a severe stomach ache on a Thursday night and asked to be taken to the hospital. This should have been a real clue to us that he was really sick and hurting because getting him to go to a doctor, much less a hospital, was like pulling teeth without any anesthesia. After transfer to Bay Medical center, they did exploratory surgery to see if they could identify the problem and discovered that he had a large colon cancer. This tumor had already metastasized into other areas and had actually caused the large intestines to rupture. There had never been any indication prior to this that he had colon cancer. He was 87 years of age when this happened.

The surgeon came out and explained the situation to Janis and me. He said the options were to try and complete the surgery, clean up the infections as best as possible, and then face several days or weeks with dad in the hospital with a colostomy bag trying to recover or to make dad as comfortable as possible for the next 24 to 48 hours and let nature take its course. That was a moment that no one wishes to face, especially when you hear that kind of news about your dad, your hero, your rock, your ......

However, as hard as it was to hear, it was an easy decision to make. Not in terms of knowing the loss that was coming but in terms of absolutely knowing what my dad would have wanted. He had made it very clear to us many times over the last few months he did not want any heroic measures taken to save his life. He was ready to go. So, we made the call, shed many tears as we held on to each other and began the wait for the inevitable.

Just as the doctor predicted, the end came within 24 hours. He passed immediately after a pastor and some dear friends said a prayer for him. He was ready for eternity. God must have been ready for him.

In spite of the difficulties that we endured during the last few months of his life, I miss him. I will never be able to fully explain how much my dad meant and means to me. He taught me so many things about life. He provided the anchor for our entire family. His wit was quick. His strength when young was almost legendary in our community. His tongue was sharp when necessary. His will (hard headed and stubborn to the nth degree) was unbroken. He was, as they say, the man.

Over the last few years, I have come to appreciate more and more the blessings of God and the life that I have been given. But, when given the chance to tell anyone about the best blessing that I ever received from God, I know exactly what to say. It goes something like this.

God has been so good to me. He has given me blessings beyond measure in ways that I can't even begin to describe and certainly do not deserve. But, the best blessing that he gave me, especially as I began my life's journey, was that He saw fit to let me be born in the home of James Quincy Lee and his wife, my mother, Gertrude M. Lee. I thank God every day for my parents and the life they gave to me.

It would be a much better world if all children in this world were as blessed as I in this regard.

Chapter 45

WAITING ON THE BIG ONE
AND BLESSED TO BE ALIVE

Today, October 6, 2014, it has been exactly four weeks since I had emergency open-heart bypass surgery to correct a major blockage in the main cardiac artery that, according to cardiologist Dr. Ben Craven and cardiac surgeon Dr. John Streitman was so severe that had I actually had a heart attack based on the condition of the blockage, it would very likely have been fatal immediately with little chance for recovery, even had the attack occurred while in a hospital or other medical care facility. The manner in which this discovery was made was only by the grace of God and his watchful care over me. I am blessed to still be alive and re- covering from this major surgery.

The process by which all of this happened began in the summer, June or July, when I decided it was time for me to visit my family doctor for the purpose of obtaining base line information on my overall health. I had not had a physical or been to a doctor in a couple of years so I decided to do this because I was in fact overweight, was not getting enough exercise and had turned 61 years of age. I wanted to start trying to lose some weight and also wanted to start an exercise program but just wanted to make sure that I was healthy enough to do this without risk. When I started this process, I was having no symptoms and was not aware that I had any pending issue, much less being a ticking time bomb waiting to have the big one.

Upon starting the process, I went to my family physician, Dr. Patrick Hawkins and we began a series of routine tests consisting of laboratory tests, blood work and a physical. During this process, it was determined that my blood pressure was 135 over 75 which was in the normal range and actually pretty good for a man of my age, size and weight. My cholesterol count was a little high, 205 with the "bad cholesterol" a little too high, but still nothing to be alarmed about as the standard for most people is under 200 as a total cholesterol count being okay. The only thing that showed up as maybe needing attention was my thyroid count was low by just a tad and I started taking a very low dose of thyroid medication on Dr. Hawkins advice.

Upon completion of this first series of examinations, I asked Dr. Hawkins to see if he could get me an appointment with the Dr. Ben Craven, a cardiologist in the Dothan Specialty Group at Flowers Hospital in Dothan, Alabama. Dr. Hawkins said he would try but was not sure that he could get me in with insurance coverage as I had no symptoms and had not had any cardiac issues. I then told him about a lengthy list of family members who had cardiac related issues over the years. Included in this list were both of my parents with long histories of high blood pressure before their deaths. My father had also had a stroke and my mother had to have a heart valve replacement surgery. In addition, both of my grandmothers had also had strokes late in their lives and my brother who is about 2 ½ years older than me has high blood pressure. When I gave him this background, he said he thought that would be enough to get me in to see Dr. Craven, especially given may age and the fact that I was overweight and not getting any type of exercise on a regular basis.

Just a few days later, I was called by Dr. Craven's office and told that I had an appointment to see him. When the date and time for the appointment arrived, I went to the office ready to proceed with gathering of information on my overall health status, particularly as related to my cardiac health.

When Dr. Craven first came into the examination room, he said to me, "What are you doing here?" I was sort of surprised by the question but I explained the process that I had gone through with Dr. Hawkins and informed him that I wanted to also find out about my cardiac condition as well. Upon hearing this, he said, "Well, that is probably a good idea given your age and weight even though you have no symptoms or have not had any issues according to your records." So with that introduction, we began a series of cardiac related tests including a thorough physical examination of the chest, heart and lungs and an electrocardiogram.

A few days after this initial visit, I again received a call from Dr. Craven's office, this time informing me that he wanted me to perform a stress test and have an echocardiogram. Upon hearing this, I asked did he think there might be some issues or were these tests just more information gathering. I was told that the electrocardiogram had shown a minor blip, nothing to be concerned about, but that he wanted the additional information that would be provided by these additional tests. Sometime during this process, Dr. Craven told me that minor blip had indicated I may have had a small hole in my heart, but upon another thorough examination, he stated emphatically that I certainly did not have a hole in my heart. So, we made the appointment for the tests on Tuesday morning, September 2, 2014, the day after Labor Day.

Bright and early on that Tuesday morning, I was in the office getting prepared for the stress test and echocardiogram.

The stress test was a nuclear stress test in which they inject a dye into your circulatory system before the test begins. In addition to the part of the stress test in which you walk on a treadmill for a length of time until your heart rate reaches the desired level or you dang well pass out, whichever comes first, they also take a series of pictures of your heart and circulatory system with a specialized camera that shows how the blood is flowing throughout your body. I guess the dye they give you lights you up like a Christmas tree on the inside so they can see how the circulatory system is working. I also had to have the echocardiogram performed which is just like a sonogram a pregnant woman would have but it is done on the heart that shows the heart function, the valves opening and closing, the blood flow through the heart and the pumping capacity of the heart. Anyway, upon completion of all of these tests, the nurse looked over my information and said to go home and the doctor would call me in a couple of days with the results and let me know if any other tests would be needed. She gave me no cause for concern and acted as if everything was okay.

On Thursday of that week, sometime in the morning, I received another call from Dr. Craven's nurse. She said that Dr. Craven wanted me to come and have a heart catheterization performed, if I was willing to do it. Now, this sort of struck me as funny when she said if I was willing to do it. My reply to her was, "I did not think this would be one of those voluntary things to have." She replied, "Well, we can't make you have it. Most people do have it but some choose not to have it done. I said, "Well, I dang sure am not going to be one of those that don't have it done. I started this process to find out if I had any issues going on and I dang sure am not going to be walking around with some ticking time bomb about to go off and not even know it. I will be there." By the way, little did I know at this time that I did indeed have a ticking time bomb that was in danger of going off at any moment.

Not knowing that there was any significant issue, the nurse told me that I could have the procedure done on Monday morning, September 8 beginning at 7:00 a.m. or Tuesday, September 9 at either 9:30 a.m. or 10:00 a.m. Thinking like only a man could think, which was about my stomach, I asked her if this would be a "fasting" procedure. In other words, I could not eat until after the procedure was finished. I thought to myself, I have seen some of those 9:30 or 10:00 appointments in doctor's offices turn into 12:00 noon or 1:00 p.m. and I don't want to be waiting that long to eat. Besides, if I was going to have it done, I figured I might as well get it over with early in the day and take care of a couple of other items of business in Dothan since I was going to be there anyway on the day of the heart cath. So, I told her I would like to have the 7:00 a.m. appointment on Monday morning.

Monday morning at about 5:45 a.m. Mike and I left home headed for the routine heart catheterization at Flower's Hospital. Because I had no indication there were any real issues going on with my heart, I also loaded some empty chlorine jugs for pool chemicals in the back of my truck, planning to stop by the pool supply shop on the way home from the hospital. I also told Mike to remind me to go by Denny Vision and pick up some contact lenses I had ordered on our way back home. We headed out, thinking in our minds that we would be home later that day or surely by the next morning, even if Dr. Craven found a small issue or blockage that he would repair with a stint while he was doing the catheterization.

Upon arrival at the hospital and getting checked in, I was sent to the preparation area in which they give you one of those lovely hospital gowns and was instructed to remove all of my clothing, including my underwear. Because of my size and height, the gown they gave me was listed as an extra-large. However, they must have used some African pigmy tribe as the models for these gowns as the extra-large barely covered the essentials, if you understand my drift. Anyway, they did manage to find another slightly larger gown though I was soon to discover that it would not have mattered which gown I was wearing as personal modesty in a hospital flies out the window like a bird in the spring pretty quickly after being admitted.

In the preparation area, I soon discovered that one of the things they do is to shave you in places that have not been shaved in a long time, maybe never on me. I believe the only place that did not have a razor touch it during this process was my head and maybe my feet. Maybe one other location that I could mention but it would be too graphic. But, other than these few exceptions, I was the poster child for a "clean shaven man." They shaved my legs, arms, chest, underarms, back, and points in between these places.

When all of the preparations were complete, they came to move me to the catheterization lab area at about 9:00 a.m. I kissed my wife and children bye and told them I would see them in a little while, not knowing what was about to take place within the laboratory. They wheeled me down to the lab to start the process, got me situated on the table and started the heart cath. For those who may not know, the patient is awake when a heart cath is being performed. I am not sure if this is true in all cases as some people may choose to be put to sleep. But, I was awake and alert while the procedure was taking place and aware of my surroundings and what was going on.

As Dr. Craven and the team were in the process of performing the procedure, there was a sudden change of atmosphere in the room and I heard Dr. Craven say to some of the other medical personnel in the room, "Who is the surgeon that we have available?" I am not sure exactly who he was talking to but I assume it was to either another doctor, perhaps his nurse or maybe another hospital staff member familiar with heart catheterizations and heart surgery. At any rate, upon hearing this question, my sense of what was going on heightened some and I had a quick thought of, "Uh-oh! This may not be good."

Before I even had a chance to really mentally process this thought, Dr. Craven had moved from the right side of the table where he had been standing to the left side of the table, closer to me head. I could sense a change in his demeanor immediately. What he said to me next was quite shocking to hear.

He said, 'Mr. Lee, we have a serious situation here. Your main cardiac artery is 95% blocked before it even splits. This is a very dangerous situation and if you have a heart attack based on this prognosis, even while you are here lying on this table, it is likely that we would not be able to save you. It would do damage to 2/3 of your heart to the degree that you would not be able to survive it. We need to do emergency cardiac by-pass open heart surgery on you today to correct this."

Now, going in to this heart cath appointment, I had assumed that Dr. Craven thought I had some minor blockage that he would correct while doing the procedure and that I would be up and out of there in a day or so. But, he had never told me that I definitely had a blockage or any other issue. Seeing his face in the lab and hearing his voice, I am convinced that he was just as surprised as me, maybe more so, that he discovered the major problem that was lurking in my heart.

Anyway, when he told me the diagnosis, my response was, "Wow, Doc! That was not what I was expecting to hear. So, we need to do surgery today, huh?" His response was short and to the point. "Yes, we need to do it today. Like now."

I really do not know how to describe what my feelings were at this point. I did not have time to be scared though I was certainly concerned and aware of the dangers of a major heart operation. But, the matter of fact manner in which the information had been presented to me made me realize that I was in fact in a very dangerous situation and needed to have the operation quickly.

After just a few moments to let the information that he had just given to me to sink in, Dr. Craven said to me, "Now if you understand what I have said to you and are in agreement for us to proceed with plans for surgery, I have some paperwork that you will need to sign to begin the preparation process." My response was, "Well, bring it here!"

Some may consider this as light and without much thought but the truth was he had given me all of the information I needed. I had a major heart attack staring me in the face and the only hope I had was to get it corrected as quickly as possible. He brought me the paperwork and

I signed it. He then went to find Mike, Ashley, Abby, Anna, my sister Janis and other family members to give the news to them. Was that ever a change of plans for all of us? What had begun as a routine day at the hospital for a routine heart catheterization procedure had just evolved into a pending major open heart surgery with little notice and no time for anyone to prepare.

Upon getting the paperwork completed and finishing up with the heart catheterization procedure, the medical team transported me to another part of the hospital to begin getting me ready for surgery. Though I am not sure about the time, I believe it was about 9:45 a.m., maybe 10:00 a.m. when this happened as the heart catheterization took about an hour.

Now to be very honest, I do not remember much about what happened or where I was once this process began. I do know that where ever I went, Mike and the girls did not see me once I went to the heart catheterization lab except for a very brief passing in the hall and a quick hug and kiss until after the by-pass surgery was completed and I was in the recovery area or in the intensive cardiac care unit. I was in this other surgery preparation area from the time I was moved, again maybe around 10:00 a.m. until the open heart, by-pass surgery actually began, which I was told was about 2:00 p.m. According to what I was told, the actual surgery lasted a little more than 4 hours which means the surgery ended at about 6:15 p.m.

I do not remember anything about the surgery or recovery except I do remember when they were either putting in or taking out the breathing tube. At some point in this, the person who was, I believe inserting the tube, had it pushed up against the back of my throat and I was unable to breathe. It felt like I was about the choke and cause me to have a gag reflex, which caused me to sort of panic for a moment. I do not know how they got it corrected or properly placed or if it was just some of the time between consciousness and being out of it caused by the anesthesia. I just remember it was not pleasant.

The first thing I remember after the surgery was being in the ICC Unit room with Mike in there with me early on Tuesday morning. I remember that Joe Taylor and my sister Janis came into the room very early to check on me. My ol' hard hearted, hard headed, man of men, dear friend Joe leaned over and planted a big old kiss on my forehead and told me he sure was glad to see me awake and alive. Janis also gave me a big kiss and hug in the short time they were allowed to be in the room. Sometime a little later in the morning, my sweet grand baby Maddie, came into the room. She had ridden the elevator up with her mom and when the doors opened, she made a bee line for my room to see her Pa even though she was not supposed to be in the unit as she was only 2 ½ years old at the time. She had brought me 2 band aides for my "boo boo" from home, holding them in her hand from Chipley to Dothan. She insisted on placing the band aids on my red heart-shaped pillow to help me get better. They stayed on the pillow until it was washed after I was released from the hospital and brought home. This little angel is loved by her Pa and this made my day to have her come to visit and take care of my "boo boo."

Later Tuesday, as I continued the process of recovering from the surgery, some of the trauma from the process began to show up. As might have been expected, I was very sore in the whole chest area which had been split open about 8 inches long right down the center. I was also very sore in my back and shoulders from where the surgeon had pried open my chest in order to do the actual surgical procedure of repairing my heart. I was also sore on my leg where they had harvested the veins used in the by-pass procedure. But, even with this, I was thankful to be alive and doing about as well as could have been expected following major cardiac surgery.

One of the side effects that I had from the surgery or maybe the anesthesia was my body temperature controls were crazy. In the first few days following surgery, I was burning up, not with a fever but just hot as heck and sweating like a hog. I had the room thermostat set at about 65 degrees and I had them bring me a fan to blow on me day and night. Mike was freezing to death wrapped up in blankets and I was burning up. I would kick the covers off me and let the fan just blow on me. Dressed in that beautiful gown I was wearing, which barely covered the essentials, I probably showed off more than I should have, if you know what I mean. But modesty had gone out the window anyway when they brought me back to the room so to heck with it. I was hot!! Anyway, about Friday, my body temperature regulator finally started getting back to normal and Mike was very glad about that.

On Wednesday following surgery on Monday, I continued to experience some pain in the area where my chest had been opened up. I was also very sore from the tubes that had been placed in my chest area during surgery to help drain excess fluid from around my lungs and to help prevent pneumonia. These really became uncomfortable during the day and when one of the doctors was making his rounds, I asked him about the tubes being removed. He told me to speak with the surgeon about this so, when his partner came into the room, I asked. He told me I was doing well and they would remove the tubes if I continued to do well later that afternoon.

Sometime around 3:00 p.m. or maybe a little later, he returned to the room and informed me he was going to be removing the tubes from my chest. When he was talking to me about removing the tubes, he said, and I quote, "This is going to be uncomfortable. It won't last long, but it will be uncomfortable." Hearing this, I asked him if I needed to get me a piece of leather to chew on while he was removing the tubes. He laughed and said I might need some. Anyway, he helped me remove the beautiful gown so that he could get to the tubes to remove them.

As he started to pull the first tube out, his warning of "This is going to be uncomfortable." does not even begin to come close to an adequate description of the pain this brief procedure caused. The tubes were not very large, perhaps a little smaller than a finger but they felt like they were about 4 inches in diameter and made out of corrugated sewer pipe when they were being removed. The entire procedure of tube removal lasted only about 30 seconds or so. But, during this 30 seconds, my eyes crossed with the pain and I would have started cursing if I would have had the forethought to engage my mouth.

A couple of days later, I told the doctor that saying "This is going to be uncomfortable." to describe the pain would be like saying "The Mississippi River is a little creek that runs down through the middle of the country from Canada to the Gulf of Mexico." to describe one of the world's great rivers. But, I survived this part of the ordeal, none the worse for wear other than the memory of the short burst of pain from the procedure.

For the remainder of the week, I started feeling a little better each day and started taking walks around the halls of the cardiac care unit. At first, I could only go a short distance but by the end of the week, I was able to make several trips down the hall each day. Of course, part of the reason for the progress was the constant reminders from Mike and others that I needed to get up and walk. In particular, one day Janis was there and insisted that I get up and walk several times. I even referred to her as "Nurse Ratchet" from the movie "One Flew Over the Cookoo's Nest" in which a really bad nurse treated the patients under her care in a heartless and mean manner. But, I know this is what helped to get me back on my feet so I guess I owe "Nurse Ratchet" a big thanks for her insistence on getting me walking and back on my feet.

By Saturday, I was really getting ready to go home or either possibly to a short stint in a cardiac rehab program. It was decided by the doctors that I was doing well enough to go home and have home health care do the follow-up visits and provide the physical therapy necessary to get me stronger and able to exercise and walk longer distances without the need to go to a rehab center. This was fine with me and it was decided that I would be released on Sunday to go home.

I must also say a great big thanks to my wife for being with me every minute from the time going to get the heart catheterization on Monday morning until I was released on Sunday afternoon. She was a real trooper and took good care of me even when I was most likely ill and not the best patient in the world. But, she hung in there and made sure that I was as comfortable as possible and made sure I received good care from the hospital staff. She was also right there with me when the staff would come in every couple of hours, day and night, to check vital signs, weigh me, or give me meds.

I was released from Flowers Hospital at about 12:30 p.m. on Sunday, September 15, 2014. My sister Janis picked me up in her SUV for a more comfortable ride home. Upon being released, we made a stop at Jimmy John's Restaurant where she bought us a sandwich and a drink for lunch. Though this was not a full, gourmet meal, it certainly beat the heck out of the hospital food that I had been served for the previous week.

We finally made it home about 2:00 or so and as soon as I got home, I went directly to my shower and took the first really good shower that I had been able to have in several days. Though making the trip home and taking a shower does not sound like a big deal, if fact I was totally exhausted from this. When I got out of the shower, I made the trip to my chair and crashed.

It still amazes me how much a major surgery impacts your overall body strength and stamina for a long time. Before the surgery, I was able to do pretty much anything I wanted to do. For the 3 weeks I had to stay out of work after getting home from the hospital, my progress was gradual but steady. I started out being able to walk only a few laps around the living room 5 or 6 times a day to the point that I was able to walk outside for a little bit up and down the roads around the house by the end of the 3 week period. Even with this progress, I had absolutely no reserve energy when I became tired or fatigued. When I "hit the wall", I was done and it took me a long time to recover.

By the end of the 3rd week at home, I was getting antsy to go back to work even though Dr. Craven wanted me to stay home another 2 weeks.

But, I convinced him I was ready to return to work on a limited basis and he agreed for me to do this if I would start with partial days and work up to full days. I started back to work on October 6 on a part time basis and was back working full time by October 20.

To say the least, major heart surgery is quite an ordeal. I am thankful to Dr. Craven and his staff for the excellent care they provided during the time leading up to the surgery and following. I am also thankful to Dr. John Streitman and his staff for their excellent care during and after surgery including the follow-up visits. And, the care and compassion of the entire staff at Flowers Hospital was beyond great as all of the nurses and staff did everything in their power to make my stay as comfortable as possible while making sure that my medical needs were met to the highest degree possible.

I can't say that I would recommend major heart surgery to any of my friends or loved ones. But, in retrospect, I am very thankful for the many professional medical care personnel who helped me to overcome this issue and put me on the road to good health.

Once I was home, I continued to make progress on my physical condition and gradually increased my exercise until I was able to walk about a mile without any issues or discomfort. After a month, I was released to start driving and after 3 months, I was allowed to start other exercises such as light upper body exercises and even allowed to begin lightly swinging a golf club again chipping and putting. Finally about the end of December, I was able to swing a golf club fully and hit full shots and got to play a full round of golf in early January.

For those who know me, I have been an avid golfer for years and love to play the game. For many years, I have been blessed to have been able to play with a fair degree of skill with a handicap in the single digits and most of the time shooting scores in the mid-to-high 70s. When I was playing regularly, if I had shot a score in the 80s, I would have not been pleased and in fact, would have been pretty hacked off. But, the first time I was able to play golf after the surgery, having not played for several months, I shot a smooth 89. I broke 90 but barely. However, on this day, I was thrilled to just play golf, enjoy the outdoors, laugh and enjoy the company of my playing partner and happy to have been blessed to be alive and able to play the game again, no matter the score.

After a few more weeks, I was able to walk 2 to 3 miles per day and even competed in (showed up and finished) a 5K run (walk with a little jogging) for the first time in my life. It was great just to be there.

In conclusion, I am happy to be alive and doing well. God blessed me by allowing me to find out about this major health issue and have it repaired before I had a heart attack which would most likely have been fatal. I am walking and/or exercising every day except for a few bad weather days or scheduling conflicts. I have lost about 35 to 40 pounds and plan to continue trying to lose more weight gradually and in a healthy way. I plan to try and make sure that I watch my health more closely in the years ahead and take better care of myself.

Though the surgery was a success and I have done well, I do not want to do it again in the near future. This is a real case of having been there and done that.

Chapter 46

POEM – "A DAY IN LIFE"

A DAY IN LIFE

Early in the morning, when the sun is on the rise,
It seems we have a lot of time for living out our lives.
What's the hurry? What's the rush? Times a' plenty so it seems.
Between the early morning dawn and the dreaming of our dreams.

But the day keeps moving onward and the morning turns to noon.
Time moves too quickly, evening will be here soon.
The sun continues sliding towards the ending of the day
And what once seemed time a' plenty now quickly fades away.

The shadows are growing longer,
The sun is sinking low
We think about the places we could have gone
But to which we didn't go.

We think about what might have been,
All the things we could have done

But the nighttime gathers round us
With the setting of the sun.

Darkness, the moon, the cool, crisp air, stars twinkling in the sky
Are reminders to the senses that the time for sleep is nigh.
The plans and dreams from early morn will forever be undone
Because our days will be completed with the setting of the sun.

ABOUT THE AUTHOR

Bill Lee was born and raised on a family farm in Bonifay, Florida that his paternal grandparents homesteaded in about 1912 and which is still in the family today. He is married to his wife of 43 years, Frances M. Lee and they have 3 children and 8 grandchildren (so far).

He enjoys many outdoor activities including fishing, hunting, golf and travel. He is also very proud of having had the opportunity to be raised on the farm by his parents, Quincy and Gertrude Lee, and the extended family of grandparents, aunts and uncles who were great influences on his life while growing up.

He has worked in public education for the last 40+ years as a teacher, coach, school principal and district administrator and is an avid supporter of public education.

He has a strong belief in the United States of America and believes the core values taught to him by his parents such as faith in God, patriotism, hard work, honesty, family and friends are the keys to leading a successful life and helping to make our world a better place for all of humanity.

Made in the USA
Columbia, SC
18 November 2023

26711163R00134